THE TEMPLE OF HEKATE

Published by Avalonia

BM Avalonia, London, WC1N 3XX, England, UK

www.avaloniabooks.co.uk

The Temple of Hekate
© Tara Sanchez, 2011
All rights reserved.

First Published by Avalonia 2011
ISBN 978-1-905297-49-8

Typeset and design by Satori
Cover Art by Georgi Mishev © 2011

British Library Cataloguing in Publication Data. A catalogue record for this book is available from the British Library.

ABOUT THE AUTHOR

Once upon a time there was a little girl who took all the other children in the street seriously when they said that if you went to the playground at midnight and skipped around the swings backwards three times the fairies would appear. So she set her alarm, snuck out the house and did as she had been instructed, the other children never did believe her when she recounted her tale. But as a result that little girl grew up to be only a slightly bigger girl with very wild hair and sometimes rather wild eyes who never stopped searching for fairies in the playground and trolls under bridges, and who harkened to things that went bump in the night and often pondered the source of those half whispered secrets in the quiet time just between wakefulness and sleep.

In her twenties she embarked on a quest to find the meaning of life the universe and everything and was rather alarmed to discover that indeed one answer could be the number 42, it has been pretty much going downhill since then.

Tara is a Torchbearer of the Covenant of Hekate, and previously contributed to the anthology *Hekate: Her Sacred Fires* (2010). She was also one of the key facilitators of the *Rite of Her Sacred Fires* (2010) with Sorita d'Este, a worldwide ceremony which was held for the first time during the Full Moon of May 2010 with participants from all over the world joining in lighting a flame for the Goddess Hekate.

Although Kentish Maid by birth (NOT a Maid of Kent) Tara currently resides on the Cheshire/Derbyshire border with her long suffering husband, beautiful and precocious daughter and a gaggle of cats and can often be discovered getting pixie led in the peaks or spinning on her beloved spinning wheel, one day she may actually get some proper work done. She is always happy to correspond with anybody genuinely interested in the Mysteries and can be contacted by email at the following address:

enquiries@templeofhekate.net

You can also write to the author:

Tara Sanchez
c/o Avalonia
BM Avalonia
London
WC1N3XX
United Kingdom

THE TEMPLE OF HEKATE

EXPLORING THE GODDESS HEKATE THROUGH RITUAL, MEDITATION AND DIVINATION

BY TARA SANCHEZ

PUBLISHED BY AVALONIA

ACKNOWLEDGEMENTS

"I cannot grasp the greatness of that One so as to attribute a greater greatness to the rest. When I see the Three together, I see but one Torch, and cannot divine or measure the undivided light"[1]

I would like to mention the following wonderful, generous and inspirational people who helped me finish this project.

The very brave Sorita d'Este who listened to an idea discussed late one night and told me to go for it, and then supported me when I did.

The incredibly talented Georgi Mishev, whose images of Hekate never fail to astound me; and who provided the cover artwork for this book.

The charming Yuri Robbers, who took the time to provide wonderful modern translations of some very old hymns, and all for the price of a *'Black Dog'*.

My dear friend Katherine Runciman, who has stood by me through some of my more hare-brained moments both magickally and mundanely, and came up trumps with some of the diagrams when my own artistic muse failed me.

My partner in crime Jonny Cole, always a source of inspiration and amusement, who was my muse and sounding board on more than a couple of occasions, his contribution to the *'Eyes of Heaven'* ritual was greatly appreciated.

Last but my no means least my wonderful husband and beautiful daughter who gave me the time and the space to work and who have tolerated me wandering around the house in my pyjamas and muttering to myself way more than usual.

There are many other souls who I would like to mention, but to thank every person who has helped me or influenced me in my journey towards the completion of this book would take a very long time, some have walked with me for just a mile, and some poor fools have signed up for the full marathon, but regardless of the distance we have travelled, the journey has been one lit by the torches of Hekate.

Thank you all.

---

[1] Gregory of Nazianzus, Oratio 40.41, C4th CE.

TABLE OF CONTENTS

Dedicated to C.
The light of my life and the darkness of my desire,
without your love and patience this book
would never have been written.

"For from Him leap forth both thunderings inexorable, and the fire-flash
receiving bosoms of the all fiery radiance of father begotten Hekate."
The Chaldean Oracles by G.R.S. Mead (trans)

FOREWORD

I started my magickal career much the same way as most people do with an interest in the unusual, the paranormal and the occult, always with one question burning strongly in my mind, *'Why?'* A question that still burns deeply at the very essence of my being even to this day, for I firmly believe that the day I stop asking is the day that I finally come face to face with the divine on an equal standing or more likely have shuffled off this turn on the merry go round and am preparing for my next incarnation.

Like many newcomers to this particular life choice my thirst for knowledge was insatiable, I quickly acquired a library full of books on every conceivable subject, from traditional witchcraft to ceremonial magick and folklore to herbalism. But whilst the books on herbs would quite clearly give you step by step instructions on how to prepare a tincture or decoction, the more esoteric books often left me feeling that the author had deliberately obfuscated the practicalities of certain subjects. And as a result I added another question to my arsenal, now I had *'how'* as well as *'why'* and I started seeking out practical experiences wherever I could so as to understand the mechanics as well as the theory.

I wrote at some length as to how my relationship with Hekate came into being, in *Hekate: Her Sacred Fires*, but for those who have, as yet to read that excellent anthology, my relationship with her is the direct result of one of these practical experiences. But it occurred to me just today whilst writing this foreword that it might actually all be Hermes' fault, some months prior to the escapades that led me to Hekate, I had prepared an extended working consisting of a series of reduction sigils which had to be drawn and then burnt at certain hours on a succession of Wednesdays; petitioning Hermes to give me knowledge and understanding on the occult arts, and it seems he took me quite seriously and provided me with possibly the best teacher of the Mysteries a girl could ask for.

As a result of the sometimes not so tender ministrations of Hekate, I have interacted with Goetic spirits, Enochian Angels, familiars both constructed and otherwise, genius loci, elementals and a whole bunch of complex individuals I am not even sure I could categorise anymore than to say they are Fae. And she has certainly shown me many *'how's'* and revealed more than a few *'why's'* along the way and for that I will forever be grateful; even if she did give me a whole more *'why's'* in the process and I cannot perceive a time in my life when I would wish to continue this journey without her supervision and valuable insights.

It appears that I am not the only person who has been so taken by her, Hekate it seems has captured the hearts and minds of generation after generation, playwrights, poets and artists have been inspired by her, men of science have tried to categorise her, holy men have embraced her mysteries or vilified her; and wherever she wills she evokes the most powerfully emotional, often primal, responses. For some she strikes terror into the very core of their being, yet for others she engenders nothing but profound respect and devotion, love almost.

For Hekate is possibly one of the most complex, multifaceted and astounding Goddesses to have ever graced the earth with her presence, her guises are too many to count and her story has spanned millennia and yet somehow still manages to remain relevant even to this day.

Facts about Hekate are relatively easy to come by, there is a whole host of knowledge out there from academics and devoted followers alike to discover and study; and it is most certainly an aspect of your craft that should not be ignored, if for no other reason than it can help to keep you sane, keep you real; time spent studying the ancient texts, scouring the sources, painstakingly translating and piecing together the fragments can be immensely fulfilling both mentally and believe it or not spiritually too, and for those dedicated souls who choose to spend their life working with her this way; it becomes a passion, an obsession almost. However, when approaching her for the first time this information can appear overwhelming, especially if you do not previously have experience of drawing from source texts to create ritual and daily practise. And so very little is written specifically about how to work with her, how to call upon her, how to create a living, workable and very personal magickal practice.

I have for a long time been conscious of the difficulty that exists for the newcomer, especially those who may not have access to local (and reputable) occult bookshops, moots and open circles etc. And for many years I turned a deaf ear and a blind eye to the bull fed to newcomers about it all being *'part of the mysteries'* and *'when the student is ready the teacher will appear'* and other such trite diatribes designed to leave the newcomer feeling inadequate and the speaker often sounding far more experienced than they really are. I always said that when it was my turn to pass what I had learnt on I would not condone such antics, my students would have to work hard of that they could be certain, and fools and time wasters would not be tolerated, but hoop jumping to learn lessons which should be gifted gladly would never be part of my curriculum, it seems Hekate might have been listening just a little too closely for one night as I ran these thoughts and ideas through my head for the 50 millionth time, an all too familiar voice said *'write a book'.*

I chose to ignore the edict to start with, but not-so chance encounters occurred and friendships were made and it became increasingly obvious that I would be nagged from here until the next life if this book didn't happen; it started its life quite humbly enough as a booklet to accompany a weekend workshop, then it grew into the outline of a correspondence course but before that could ever come to fruition a late night discussion gave birth to something bigger.

What I have attempted to achieve with this book is to provide a framework, an exemplar of what can be done, and how. As an old mentor once said to me, I can give you a map, but the map is not the whole territory. This is a map, but along the journey this map portrays you may find many other things to explore, side roads previously undiscovered. In fact everything in this book is the culmination of doing just that, exploring the territory given to me by my magickal experiences past and present, and then creating something living and workable, it is not *the* way it is *a* way and should be approached as such, a resource from which you can build something rich, expressive, and potentially life changing.

Tara Sanchez
Cheshire 2011

A VERY BRIEF INTRODUCTION

The earliest and most comprehensive surviving text that references Hekate was written by Hesiod, a shepherd cum poet from Boetia. In his work *Theogony* (quite literally meaning *'birth of the Gods'*), which dates to somewhere between the 8th and 7th century BCE, he presents a fairly complete cosmology or mythical worldview starting with the creation of the earth and the reign of the Titan Gods and effectively ending with the Olympian Gods.

Within this work Hesiod describes how Zeus, the head of the Olympian Gods, leads a rebellion against the older Titan Gods who were their progenitors; and he promises anybody that aids him in his battle against the Titans would retain all that was theirs in the old order, Hekate it seems took up this offer and fought with the Olympians. A fact that many have chosen to ignore, and have tried to read into this instead that Hekate was somehow very special to Zeus; and whilst to have control over both earth, sea and sky is pretty impressive and far more powerful than you would think Zeus would want a former *'enemy'* to retain, you have to note that *"all this she has as her due portion"*.[2] This means nothing extra was given; this wasn't an act of favouritism, he was just keeping his side of the bargain.

In fact the powers accorded to Hekate were fairly extensive and are not specifically elemental, they include the judgement of kings, aiding victory in battle, success in sporting activities, aiding horsemen, helping sailors, fishermen, farmers and shepherds and the successful reproduction of livestock and guardian to the new born; and yet upon closer study of subsequent mythology and papyri fragments; there is one glaring oddity. This veritable powerhouse amongst the Gods has no mythology of her own; she at best only plays bit parts in other tales. This then leads onto the question of whether Hekate was of *'Greek'* origin at all!

If Hekate was a foreign Goddess brought over from Asia Minor and adopted into the Greek Pantheon, then it would explain her lack of mythology. But where in Asia Minor this might have been, scholars are split, some believe she actually originated from Thrace and was adopted by the people of Asia Minor first, before her emigration into the Greek empire. Others believe her origins to be Karian.

It has also been posited that she may have even come from as far afield as Mesopotamia, which in theory may go some way to explain the much quoted but totally unproven theory that is held dear by so many neo-pagans that she is a later incarnation of the Egyptian frog-headed Goddess Heqet, which would go some way to tying her more closely to the Hekate of the *Chaldean Oracles*. However at this time there appears to be little or no physical or literary evidence to support this; so the only thing we really know

---

[2] Theogony, Hesiod, C8th-C7th BCE.

for sure is that, her journey most probably began far from Olympus and the children of Kronos.

So why would a foreign Goddess be so readily accepted into a well established and pre-existing pantheon? It is possible that this happened because she was sufficiently similar in her aspects that she filled a gap of a long lost but not quite forgotten deity still lingering in the cultural consciousness of the peoples of Ancient Greece. It is also possible that she is the remaining fragment of an indigenous Neolithic or early Bronze Age Goddess given a new name and a bit of a makeover. There are a couple of fairly obvious candidates for this role and the table below details briefly who they are and what roles they fulfilled.

Name	Meaning	Era/Region	Symbols	Mythology
Bendis	Unknown	Thrace	Twin Lances Twin Torches	Goddess of the Moon and Hunting possibly the Thracian equivalent of Artemis
Britomartis	Sweet Maid Virgin	Minoan	Associated with Potnia Theron, Mistress of the Labyrinth	Beloved of Artemis and rescued from death, reminiscent of Iphigenia who became Hekate
Snake Goddess	Unknown	Minoan	Snakes held aloft in a manner similar to the twin torches of Hekate	Unknown

HEKATE, GREEK MAGICK & RELIGION

> *"Many definitions of the word magic have been attempted: none, perhaps is wholly satisfactory"*[3]

Magick is such a nebulous thing, put a dozen witches, pagans, occultists and magicians in a room and ask them to define magic and you will get two dozen answers. Over the years many people have tried to define magick and whilst all the definitions are probably true they often conflict, leaving the questing soul wondering where it was that they missed the point. One of my most favourite quotes of all time sums this phenomenon up rather nicely, *"The opposite of a fact is falsehood, but the opposite of one profound truth may very well be another profound truth."* It was made by the renowned Physicist Niels Bohr who was, after a fashion, as much a philosopher as a man of science, and it is probably the one overriding tenet by which I live my life, for to argue that it is otherwise is the route to dogma, stagnation and failure to progress.

---

[3] Magic in Greek and Latin Literature, Lowe, 1929.

Lowe perhaps has the right idea, for we do feel a need to categorise, label, and define our world around us in a logical manner that is *'true'* for us. In his study of magick in Greek and Roman literature he attempts to classify rather than define works of magick. Broadly speaking, he splits them into acts of black and white magick under the categories of religious or sympathetic magick, where the sympathetic magick is purely a mechanical act that requires no intervention from a higher being or supernatural power other than the practitioner's own will.

Others have also made this distinction by using the terms *'low'* and *'high'* magick, where the act of sympathetic magick is considered *'low'* and the ceremonial and religious is considered *'high'*. In my opinion this approach is not only fairly arrogant, it is in essence a falsehood for there are instances in ancient texts and Grimoires of the learned and religious magician performing acts of sympathetic magic without the coercion of spirits, and equally there is evidence of the humble pellar/cunning man/witch creating charms which rely on the good will or the evocation of a greater power or spirit for the success of the operation.

This blurring of definition existed even in ancient times and Lowe suggests that, *"Though the official priest of a savage god may use magic in his appeal to that deity, he is not a wizard. It is the unofficial practitioner who is a witch, just as the unqualified medical practitioner is a quack"*,[4] which does make sense. But even this has its exceptions, for Medea, arguably the most famous of the Thessalian witches, served as a Priestess at the temple of Hekate. Therefore it could be argued that as a serving priestess her acts were *'official'* and they were most certainly religious, for she (and other witches of her ilk in classical literature) calls upon Hekate regularly to aid her in her rites. Also archaeological and literary evidence shows that the common man would honour the Gods both in the temple and the domestic sanctuary giving offerings to their patron deity and other domestic deities, thus performing acts of a religious nature and in some cases, the act of magic themselves.

> *"Each month at the new moon he cleaned and crowned his Hermes and his Hekate and all the rest of the sacred objects (or 'shrines,' hiera) that his ancestors left behind, and he honoured them with offerings of incense, barley cakes (psaistoi) and roundcakes (popanoi)."*[5]

Spells and magick, both black and white (and it was often black – cursing, binding and necromancy being quite common) were essentially a part of everyday life and would probably not have even been called magick at all. So my only conclusion is, that it is the manner in which the act is performed that differentiates between sanctioned and acceptable magickal acts and the dubious incantations of the nefarious witch. Perhaps for Medea her faux pas was to operate outside the system, away from the temple or the domestic sanctuary and without the knowledge of her father, thus earning her the title of witch; and for others such as the witches Canidia and Sagana

---

[4] Magic in Greek and Latin Literature, Lowe, 1929.

[5] De Abstinentia, 2.16, Porphyry, C4th CE.

the title was earned because they performed their malevolent arts in a place of taboo, the graveyard.

The ancient world was after all, fairly preoccupied with the dead, in what appears to be pretty much a love-hate relationship; they seemed to spend an inordinate amount of time either appeasing them so they would stay away or summoning them for help and guidance. The improperly buried, those who suffered untimely or dishonourable deaths, were in particular avoided unless absolutely necessary. Virgil illustrates the importance of a proper burial quite clearly in the *Aeneid*, his hero Aeneas whilst journeying to the underworld comes across a host of departed souls on the earthly side of the river Styx. The Sybil, who was also sometimes considered an initiated priestess of Hekate, informs him that they are unable to cross as Charon the ferryman can only carry those that have received proper burial.

It is perhaps no coincidence then that Horace placed the statue of Priapus who stands in the cemetery frequented by the acolytes of Hekate, Canidia and Sagana, in a burial site that was less than desirable, *"Once slaves paid to have the corpses of their fellows, Cast from their narrow cells, brought here in a cheap box. This was the common cemetery for a mass of paupers"*.[6] Most certainly a demographic of society that was likely to have died untimely or dishonourable deaths if ever there was one and their burials as we can deduce from the statement above would have hardly seemed proper; these would be the souls that are still trapped upon the earthly plane, for a hundred years if Virgil is to be believed.

This view that inappropriate ritual and magick was any act performed away from the public eye, in an unconsecrated space or without knowledge of the patriarch of the family unit appears to be have been held by Plato, who in his dialogue *Laws* proposes rules and regulations which should be imposed upon the Polis.

> *"Let no one possess shrines in their private houses. When anyone is moved in spirit to do sacrifice, he shall go to the public places to sacrifice, and he shall hand over his oblations to the priests and priestesses to whom belongs the consecration thereof."*[7]

He posits the outlawing of all household shrines, something that Medea quite clearly states she maintains, in the eponymous play by Euripides. But even more condemnatory is his reasoning behind such a law, naming fraudulent sorcerers and women who maintain multiple and ill-conceived household shrines as the main culprits for impious behaviour.

We cannot know however, for definite, if the theories discussed above are the actual reason for the demonisation of certain practises and the reduction of the practitioners to the status of witch; but there is a fairly strong argument to suggest that magick was only considered magick and therefore something less than desirable if it was performed inappropriately.

What I have done over the years is study these texts and learn what I can from them. It was not my calling to reconstruct faithfully every minutiae or detail for I live in a modern world and our modern culture does not really

---

[6] Satire VIII, Horace, 35 BCE.
[7] Laws, 909d, Plato, C4th BCE.

share the same taboos as those in the ancient world, as a daughter I was not my father's property until I married and my views of the dead are not quite so maudlin, I do not fear that phantoms of the dead will haunt me in my sleep to the detriment of my health. For much of what would have been called magick now falls firmly into the realms of science and medicine, it would be foolish of me for example, to take a bean with a bug in it and make an amulet, as suggested in one of the *Greek Magical Papyri* spells, and use this as my only method of contraception, when a trip to the family planning clinic is a far more effective and sensible option.

So, much of what might have been considered *'magick'* in the ancient world is far from it today, however the classifications do in many ways still hold true, religious and sympathetic magic still exists. Sympathetic magick can be and in fact is, practised by anybody who cares to learn the art. Religious magick can also be performed by those who have the calling, but with the advent of neo-paganism what would have been considered as inappropriate unsanctioned religious magick is quite possibly even more rife than it was in ancient times, for with the exception of certain modern western mystery traditions there is no established *'system'* within which a person can operate; no easily accessible priesthood in which to enter whether it be for religious, socio-political or economic reasons and neither are priestly roles conferred as a hereditary right.

This does not however mean we should not practise religious magick, for the one lesson we can learn from our study of the ancient world is that, with the exception of certain mystery cults, such as those of Eleusis, service to the Gods was truly of the people. In essence, any person could become a priest or priestess, with some notable conditions such as being free from physical defect, or having one's virginity intact when serving certain virgin Goddesses. Indeed there are recorded cases of priesthoods being auctioned off to the highest bidder. Service in the priesthood need not be a lifelong vocation either, it was quite common for there to be a fixed term of service, after which the position would be conferred to another, who was often elected by the community.

It is also important to note that the key function of the priesthood was not always specifically one of intercession with godhead, although this was undeniably a part, it was as much a role, a job, one that primarily focused on both service to the deity and the community around. One could almost liken it to a facilitator, it was necessary for someone to know the appropriate prayers, how to perform the correct libations and sacrifices, ensure the cleanliness of the sanctuary and tally the temple accounts, tend sacred plants and trees, even create certain annually required ritual artefacts. In fact the titles chief cook, bottle washer and general lackey spring to mind when studying the diverse duties of the priesthood in ancient Greece, and so it is today for those who choose to take on the title of priest or priestess.

There was and to some extent still is prestige and status conferred as a result of undertaking the obligations of priesthood. In ancient times there were certain rewards for this hard work and dedication, gifts of food, skins, offerings that never made it to the main altar due to space constraints, some temples even levied charges for performing certain services, and whilst the majority of this coinage would have gone towards the upkeep of the temple sanctuary, the priesthood would upon occasion receive a stipend, a fair day's pay for a fair day's work. Rather a far cry from the overwhelming modern neo-pagan opinion that no monies should be taken for training or works undertaken.

CONCEPTS OF HEAVEN AND HELL

As we have already briefly touched upon the preoccupation with the dead in the ancient world, it would be remiss not to at least attempt to understand the basics of the doctrine surrounding the afterlife, especially as it was and still is, so closely connected to Hekate.

The Greek concept of the afterlife is relatively simple and certainly should not be alien to anyone who has spent some time seriously considering their own beliefs and the beliefs of others. But it does have a few interesting nuances, as already mentioned, how one was buried could affect where you ended up, how you lived your life and any interference by the Gods could also have a profound effect on what came next. They would not have totally understood the Christian ideals of heaven and hell however, and they would have been totally confused by any broad sweeping statements associating Hades with a pit of eternal suffering where souls burnt in agony forever. Hades was in essence split into two distinct areas or districts, namely Erebus (also known as the Asphodel Plain), and Tartarus, with a third section, Elysium, reserved for the great and the good.

As long as you didn't end up as one of Hekate's horde trapped on the earthly plane, you were destined for the underworld in some form or other. Impressions of the underworld vary throughout the available literary references; Homer writes that his hero, Odysseus, is advised by Kirke the witch, to travel to the underworld as part of his epic quest to return home. To facilitate this he was advised to perform a rite of sacrifice which bears a very strong resemblance to the rite Medea advises Jason to perform to evoke the Goddess Hekate.

> *"I drew a sharp sword from my side and dug a trench as long and as wide as a man's forearm. There I poured libations to all the dead, first with a mixture of honey and milk, then with sweet wine, and last of all with water. Over all this I sprinkled some white barley."*[8]

Later he cuts the throats of a number of sheep pouring their life blood into the trench, from which the spirits in the underworld must drink before they are able to interact with the living. The location of this rite seems to be the key to access into the underworld, as it in a liminal place that is never touched by sunlight, which seems to infer a place below the earth. It appears the underworld exists almost as if it is coincident with, but slightly out of phase with the real world, for it is the sacrificial rite that makes the spirits tangible, almost as if the draining life of the animals in the rite allowed a link from which the dead could draw energy. It is described as both a house and a hall, like a residential dwelling; this description is in essence Erebus, where ordinary souls exist in the underworld.

---

[8] The Odyssey, Homer, C9th BCE.

Both Homer and Hesiod mention Tartarus as a place that exists far beneath Hades; this is essentially a prison for those who offend the Gods, including some of the Gods themselves, specifically the Titan ones. In the *Greek Magical Papyri*, Hekate is mentioned a number of times as being the ruler of Tartarus and the opener or key holder to the gates of Hades. Plutarch more radically suggests that Tartarus and Elysium may be either wholly or partially on the moon which he equates to Hekate and it is her will and judgement that decides the fate of the disembodied soul. The interesting ideas of Plutarch notwithstanding, Elysium was generally considered to be either another region apart from Erebus or an island entirely of its own away from Hades existing at the edges of the earth. Elysium is a plentiful island of milk and honey where only a select and honoured few may dwell, not dissimilar in concept to the Valhalla of Norse mythology, the place all warriors aspire to go upon their demise.

The main concept to take away from this ideology is that at certain places and at certain times it was possible to interact with the denizens of the other worlds, and we too can do the same either by finding those places that occur naturally; where the *'here'* and the *'there'* coincide or by creating them ourselves through magickal rites and calling upon the Goddess Hekate to aid us.

DAEMONS & OTHER SPIRITS

"Many are the forms taken by the plans of the Gods"[9]

The supernatural world as we would understand it was a fundamental part of Greek life and its subsequent mythology; Keres, Moirae, nature spirits such as nymphs, and heroes with demigod status and extraordinary powers were all commonplace in popular culture. There are a number of these supernatural beings which are strongly connected with Hekate in ancient literature and at least a brief study of their nature and purpose is necessary as they can strongly enhance work with Hekate herself.

THE DAEMON

Describing the essence of a daemon is actually quite difficult, in its simplest form the word means *'spirit'* and is most likely the origin of the modern word demon; which of course brings to mind images of devilish imps with tails and horns set on stealing your mortal soul and dragging it to the depths of hell. Daemons however, in ancient times were viewed quite differently and different forms of spirits were given this epithet, sometimes with little rhyme or reason, and not all were bad. They could be ancestral dead, demigods, or even the Gods themselves, who were also, from time to time, given the epithet of daemon.

---

[9] Bacchae, Euripides, C5th BCE.

If you search for a definition of a daemon, you will find that some have tried to simplify the concept into a singular type of entity, mostly benevolent, an attendant spirit almost like a guardian angel. This is not strictly untrue; Plato himself in one instance defined the daemon as a superior being whose role it was to govern humanity.

But possibly one of the most significant dialogues of Plato when considering the daemon is his dialogue *Symposium*, where he writes that Sophocles believed that love was not a God as some of the other protagonists in the work purported, but instead a great daemon. One who was neither good nor bad and who operated as intermediary between the Gods and mortal man conveying prophecy, divine instruction in magickal arts and initiations from above; and prayers, spells and sacrifices from below, the daemon was considered as being neither mortal nor divine and as such was considered in the perfect position to make the connection between the two realms.

Hesiod,[10] probably because of a lack of Chaldean influence, claimed that some of the daemons are the spirits of earlier races of men and categorised them as follows:

- The race of the men of gold, this is the earliest race of mortals purported to have lived during the reign of Kronos and the Titans. They now reside within the earth and stand as guardians, protecting from harm and bestowing wealth.

- The race of the men of silver, these mortals were created by the Olympian Gods, smaller in stature and less intelligent than the Gold. They were reckless, foolish, godless creatures who lived short lives; little is said as to their nature other than they are still honoured, but their spirits rest in the underworld.

- The race of Bronze appear to have been warlike barbaric mortals, they fought between themselves and eventually this constant warring caused the race to die out, they appear to have travelled straight to Tartarus where their spirits remain.

- The race of Heroes, who by the grace of the Gods have been transported to Elysium where they live in peace and harmony forever.

- The race of the men of iron, the current race who favour strength and do not possess honour, who are left by the Gods to fight their own battle against evil.

As we shall soon see this belief that the *'Men of Gold'* were guardians that resided within the earth and who bestowed wealth, appears on the surface to be in direct opposition to the Chaldean school of thought, but it is worth bearing in mind, as we explore this concept in just a little more detail, that there are always two sides to a story and the truth inevitably lies somewhere in between.

Hekate's connection with the Chaldean daemon spirits both beneficent and malevolent is well documented; the Chaldeans placed them in their

---

[10] Works and Days, Hesiod, C8th-C7th BCE.

hierarchical order of superior beings that were under the direct governance of the Goddess Hekate.

> *"She is the driver of the aery and the earthly and the watery dogs"*[11]

The beneficent daemons or *'dogs'* as they were sometimes called aided the magician with their work operating in a similar manner to the Men of Gold, according to Hesiod, or the daemon love as described by Plato, bringing messages and accompanying Hekate herself in the form of the Iynx when she chooses to manifest. These daemons were most often considered to be *'airy'*, which is the realm that stands between the earth and the moon, just below the realms of the Gods, and it is this proximity to the Gods that made them so uniquely qualified to perform their role. Whereas the malevolent daemons were often considered earthly and caused the magician much consternation, tricking the magician and giving false oracles; these daemons in earlier times were also considered to bring nightmares and sometimes madness.

Little is said in the *Chaldean Oracles* themselves about how you may tell the malevolent daemons apart from the beneficent ones, however, Iamblichus in his work *De Mysteriis* describes the good daemon as having a fiery form, that glows with a stable inner light whilst the bad daemon *"drags with it the signs of bonds and punishments"*.[12] A significant number of the fragments that relate to Hekate mention her appearance in connection with fire or spirits of light, which would seem to infer beneficent daemons accompanying her rather than malevolent ones. This being said there is one very interesting fragment, which may tie both the beliefs of Hesiod and the beliefs of Plato and the Chaldeans together.

> *"Nature persuades us that the daemons are pure, and things that grow from evil matter useful and good"*[13]

Here we have Physis (or Nature), who in another fragment is considered to hang from the back of Hekate clearly stating that the daemons are pure, and that even things that come from evil matter, namely the earthly realms, can be both useful and beneficent. Not all scholars agree with this assessment of this fragment, however if we look to other magickal practises over the millennia, we find malevolent, even demonic entities being used by and working with the magician for the magician's purpose, which may or may not be for the greater good. The grimoire called the *Goetia* is an excellent example of this, which is still used by magicians the world over today.

---

[11] Chaldean Oracle Fragment 45, C2nd CE.

[12] De Mysteriis, Iamblichus, C3rd CE.

[13] Chaldean Oracles, C2nd CE.

THE PERSONAL DAEMON

There is one final type of daemon to briefly examine before we move on and that is the personal daemon. Historically this was a specific daemonic entity that was responsible for directing and guiding the corporeal life of a particular soul until such point in time that the soul had developed sufficiently and was able to receive a particular deity as their patron. How this guardian daemon manifested is a little divided, some believed that it was a part of the magician themselves, effectively their higher self, the part of their soul which was made up of the cosmic world soul and assigned to them prior to the individual soul's embodiment on the material plane; whilst others believed they were distinct entities who later joined with the lucky and pious few who achieved sufficient enlightenment to receive a God as their guardian.

If this seems a little familiar to you, this is because even to this day, some magickal practitioners strive to achieve what is known as *'the knowledge and conversation of the Holy Guardian Angel'*. The magician Aleister Crowley posited that it was every magician's ultimate purpose to gain this interaction and by doing so would learn of their part in the *'Great Work'*.

The theurgic perspective was not so different, both Iamblichus and Plato believed that it was necessary to the development of the soul to identify the personal daemon and to listen to and act upon instruction given to them by the daemon. Plato even suggested that it was the mortal's actions that fed the daemon, godly divine actions effectively kept the daemon fed, whilst more base material actions would eventually lead to a separation of the mortal from the daemon spirit. This would leave the mortal wholly human and divorced from that part of their soul that was part of the cosmic world soul, this then resulted in them re-incarnating into a lower life form until they had effectively worked out whatever *'evil'* it was that caused such actions and the resultant separation. As an interesting side note, the next lowest entity after man was woman!

My own stance regarding the *'higher self'* vs. *'separate entity'* is, I will be honest, also divided. The concept of it being a discrete entity assigned to only select individuals prior to incarnation into the material realms smacks of a level of predetermined fate over and above my own personal gnosis. The theurgic view point is the one that sits most comfortably with me, that it is our personal duty for the development of our souls to identify and *'feed'* our personal daemon which is divinely gifted to us and mediates for us between the material realms and Hekate in her aspect as the Cosmic World Soul.

ANCESTRAL SPIRITS AND GHOSTS

As we discussed briefly earlier in the section entitled *Hekate, Greek Magick & Religion*, Hekate has a number of links with ancestral spirits and the restless dead, Ogden (2002)[14] suggests that normally these restless dead

---

[14] Magic Witchcraft and Ghosts in the Greek and Roman Worlds, Ogden, 2002.

fall into one of four categories: those who died before their time; those who died by violence; those that died unwed (particularly women) and those who were deprived of a proper burial. In just about all of the above cases, the soul of the deceased might either linger upon the earthly plane by its own volition or is barred from the underworld either temporarily (until appropriate action was taken by the living) or sometimes permanently.

Hekate's connection with the dead actually stems back to her early literary beginnings, when she becomes both the guide and follower of Persephone after her return to the underworld she is effectively becoming the guide of the Queen of the Underworld. Euripides mentions Hekate's ability to send phantoms against the living and as we have discussed earlier Canidia and Sagana call upon her in a graveyard whilst performing an act of necromancy. The *Orphic Hymn to Hekate* quite clearly shows her connection with the ghosts of the dead when it states that the Goddess is, *"Pleas'd with dark ghosts that wander through the shade"*.[15]

By the time of the *Greek Magical Papyri* (C2nd BCE – C5th CE) this association was complete with a number of the spells involving Hekate or a Hekate complex referring to or involving the restless dead, some of which are also rites of necromancy.

Many modern priests and priestesses of Hekate perform works of magick involving the restless dead, often aiding lost souls to *'pass over'*, however it is not an area of work that I actively pursue.

NATURAL SPIRITS

As mentioned above, the ancient Greek world was practically riddled with supernatural creatures of every shape size and description; trees, streams, seashores, caves, you name it, all seemed to have some kind of attendant spirit in situ, one has to ask oneself, if even half of these creatures were real, where did they go? Or are they still out there waiting to be rediscovered? And from personal experience I would say that they still endure and rites involving Hekate seem to attract them over and above any other rite I have ever been involved in, with perhaps the exception of rites involving *'Lake Ladies'*, but that is a whole other kettle of fish! It would be next to impossible to write about every creature in the phenomenal bestiary that is Greek myth and legend so only those that have some form of connection with Hekate have been listed and this can be found in Appendix II - *Other Magickal Creatures*.

THE WINDS

In Greek mythology there are four main winds which are assigned geographical directions, three of which were assigned to a season of the year (the Greeks originally only had three seasons). The winds were often portrayed as winged men or sometimes horses.

---

[15] Hymn to Hecate, Taylor (trans), C1st-C3rd CE.

- Boreas – The God of the North Wind, often depicted as a bearded unkempt man, associated with winter.
- Notus – The God of the South Wind, often depicted as clean shaven pouring water from a vase, associated with late summer and autumn.
- Zephyrus – The God of the West Wind, often depicted as clean shaven and youthful, associated with spring and early summer.
- Euros – The God of the East Wind, often depicted as a red headed or tawny bearded man
- Aeolus – The ruler of the winds, in some legends each wind was considered to be dangerous if allowed to roam the globe unchecked; so Zeus insisted that they each took their place in a specific region of the world, whilst in other stories they were constrained to a subterranean prison by their ruler Aeolus, and only unleashed upon the world when instructed to do so by the Gods.

The main connection with the Goddess Hekate is that of the witch Medea, who in Flaccus' *Argonautica* is accused of charming and controlling the winds by the Goddess Hera. In Ovid's *Metamorphoses*, Medea invokes Night, the Stars, the Moon, the Winds and Hekate during which Medea clearly claims that by calling the wind she controls them. And finally Pausanias mentions in his *Description of Greece* that there is in Titane, which is in the region of Corinth, an altar to the four winds, where the priest makes sacrifice to Hekate in four chthonic altars and chants the charms of Medea.

INVOKING VS. EVOKING

It's always hard to decide at what point you should start discussing the difference between invoking and evoking, too early and you can send an enthusiastic yet relatively naive seeker running for the hills, too late and confusion and misunderstanding can already be ingrained into the psyche.

Part of the confusion surrounding this subject is that many use the terms interchangeably and others are not even aware there is a difference. I was originally taught that magicians never invoke, only witches, almost as if it was somehow a lesser operation. The theory is that when one invokes there is a strong chance that total control can (and in fact possibly should) be given over to the entity you invite to share your headspace, and losing control is something a magician never does. I initially just accepted this doctrine but it became obvious to me in later years that you cannot categorise each operation under the same heading, even if the desired outcome, in this case interaction with a deity, is essentially the same. For both are separate skills and are appropriate in different circumstances, for example there are certain entities I would never invoke and there are one or two deities I would rather not evoke if I could help it.

However, from a general perspective, within any given ritual it is possible to either evoke or invoke, and which you choose to use will affect the ritual you will create. As to what each technique entails has always a topic of hot debate, for some traditions can and do use these terms interchangeably, whilst others are very specific about the meanings and when to use each term. As previously mentioned, it has been said that witches invoke and magicians evoke; and whilst that can be true it is not always the case, so what is the difference and why do one over the other? Sadly looking at the terms just linguistically in a dictionary isn't the greatest of help when clarifying the difference, the occult scholar David Rankine defines the difference rather eloquently:

> *"Both words derive from the Latin word vocare meaning 'to call', however invocation is a calling into, and evocation is a calling forth. Invocation can be considered a calling of a deity or spiritual creature into something or someone.*
>
> *This then includes the use of crystal stones, glass receptacles, bowls of liquid and magick mirrors, statues as fetishes and the Wiccan ceremony of 'Drawing Down the Moon', as well as deity possession work as seen in systems like Voodoo. Evocation is the calling forth of a spiritual creature to tangible presence, often in a triangle or other constraining space."*[16]

Invoking is generally utilised in group rites of devotion and when oracular work is being performed, where the priest or priestess effectively becomes the voice box for any oracles that the specific deity called upon may wish to impart and also for empowering or ensouling objects. Whereas, evocation is often used when the practitioner wishes to draw upon or learn from the energies of the deity being called; or to interact with them in some physical manner; whilst retaining a full level of control. It is this latter technique that the non religious magickal practitioner may wish to adopt exclusively, although there is no reason why invocation couldn't happen even if the level of belief only extends to the idea of Jungian archetypes

Historically there seems to be more of a precedent for evoking Hekate than invoking her, although some will argue that when the famous priestesses of Hekate such as Kirke and Medea called upon their Goddess and claimed that they could draw down the moon from the sky, they were in fact invoking her, there is little evidence to suggest that this was actually the case. So whilst it is common to include an invocation within acts of devotion it does not mean that you must invoke Hekate, far from it, after all when Jason gave offerings to Hekate he left before she physically manifested and the initiates that performed the rite of Hekate-Erischigal, assumed a number of body postures to ensure that the entities in the rite did not come near.

The ancient Greek relationship with deity followed a similar pattern to that of the dead, the majority of magickal operations involving them were aimed at either summoning them externally or avoiding contact with them altogether. The former is, at least initially, not a bad approach to adopt, unless you have some kind of experience in performing invocation or the back up of an experienced priest or priestess to aid you. It would be advisable to steer well clear until you have built a solid relationship with

---

[16] Private correspondence with the author, January 2011.

Hekate, for she can come across in some very surprising ways, for example, more than one or two priestesses of Hekate have reported very sensual and sexual experiences when working with her in this way.

Also many a minutely planned ritual has gone drastically astray as the result of a particularly successful invocation, where the presiding deity will take it upon themselves to give sage words of wisdom and even proverbial kicks up the backside to unsuspecting members of the group in attendance, and sometimes just generally hijack the whole ritual for their own, often undisclosed purposes. This kind of manifestation at best can be unsettling to an inexperienced group and at worst, when suddenly presented with a priestess whose voice and even appearance has suddenly warped or changed, downright scary.

PRACTICE

KEEPING A MAGICKAL JOURNAL

Many books on the occult and magick encourage you to keep a notebook or journal; the reasons for this are quite simple; despite having a phenomenal potential mental capacity, the average human uses only a fraction of their brain, and few if any of us have perfect recall.

Keeping a journal allows us to record events and information in crystal clarity whilst it is fresh in our hearts and minds for future reference.

How in depth you make this journal is of course up to you, for you can choose to include the finest of details, the type of incense used (and its recipe), the flowers decorating the altar (you could even press one or two of the type), the name of the wine that was used during the rite. The possibilities are endless. At the very least you should however record the following information each time you perform a rite honouring or including Hekate.

- Phase of the Moon
- Date
- Time
- Purpose of the Rite
- Notes and observations.

As you work through this book you may also want to include the following

- Planetary hour
- Divination type
- Divination outcome
- Personal Prayers

For the ladies reading this book you may want to record the phase of your menstrual cycle; hormonal influences can have astonishing effects, some women report that their work is more or less profound at certain times of the month and they adapt their magical working month to reflect this.

Over the years I have found the magickal journal to be a very useful tool, not just for assessing my own progress and development but also co-incidentally understanding other people's magick and motivations. However, like many practitioners I probably do not keep one as fastidiously as I ought. And more than a few rituals which should have been recorded have been consigned to the annals of my leaky memory rather than committed to paper.

This neglect tends to happen in circumstances where I am working away from home where the ritual is followed by some form of social component, and/or I am outdoors and do not wish to expose my very posh handcrafted leather journal to either the elements or prying eyes. One day I will remember that whilst a beautiful journal lovingly kept in copperplate italics is a thing of magick in its own right, a cheap note book for taking notes on the fly can be just as useful. Therefore in true parent fashion I urge you to do as I say, not as I do; by all means keep a beautiful journal, but do make sure you also have some form of rough-book for taking notes as soon as possible after the working, which you don't mind getting wet and grubby.

Another reason for journals and note taking (as well as personal practice) falling by the way side is that the write up can sometimes take as long if not longer than the ritual or meditation itself, so make sure you have adequate time laid aside. As a general rule of thumb if you plan to spend ten minutes a day doing a ritual devotion or meditation allot another twenty minutes to write it up. Lack of time though should never be used as an excuse to not undertake any magickal work, again that scrappy notebook should serve you well and you can then write everything up beautifully at your own leisure.

THE ALTAR

"Dig a circular pit. Over it slit the throat of a female sheep and burn it whole, heaping high a pyre on the very edge of the pit"[17]

The altar or *bomos* was a central part of ritual both religious and magickal in the ancient world, it was here that sacrifices and offerings to the Gods were placed and often immolated; they often stood alone in front of the main sanctuary in such a way that the congregated worshippers could stand around the altar as part of the rite.

There were two distinct types of altar, that of the high Olympian altar which was raised, and the chthonic altar which was most often a pit; dug into the earth itself with a fire built to the side. In both cases similar offerings were made to the deities although some literary evidence suggests that when an animal was sacrificed to an Olympian deity then the creatures throat was cut and the head bent back in such a way that the blood from the jugular would spurt upwards, whilst the chthonic sacrifice was made in such a way that the blood from the animal would be drained into the pit below.

There is evidence that both types of altars were used in the worship and magick of Hekate, there are archeologically three Olympian altars of note, one on the Island of Samothrace dated from sometime in the 6th century BCE, another at the Temple of Apollo in Miletus which is now in Turkey but was once the province of Ionia and finally the altar which remains in the ruins of the Temple of Hekate in Lagina. In addition to this, there is a reference to a yearly procession at Didyma which was an oracular centre of worship for Apollo similar to Delphi, that describes a procession where two stone cubes were carried and placed before a statue of *"Hekate before the gates"*, the name given to statues of Hekate which were found outside temples to other Gods. Little seems to be known about the function of these cubes but they may possibly have been some form of temporary altar for the festival.

Archaeological evidence of chthonic altars associated with Hekate is almost nonexistent, unless of course you include the subterranean cysts in Knossos where the Minoan Snake Goddess was discovered; this of course is unsurprising for holes in the ground are subject to the ravages of time far more than altars made of large slabs of rock. However, literary references abound and although we must take care to remember that many of these references are contained within works of fiction we have to make the assumption that just as in the future historians will be able to glean from

---

[17] Argonautica, 3.130-131, Apollonius of Rhodes, C3rd BCE.

the information contained within modern works of fiction much about our current lifestyle, so too can we from these historical stories and plays.

PRACTICAL EXERCISE: CREATING A DEVOTIONAL ALTAR

As a general rule it appears that acts of magick were performed in front of a chthonic altar. Jason, Kirke, Aeneas and the Cumaean Sybil all perform magickal rites using a chthonic altar, particularly rites of evocation where the Goddess herself is summoned into manifestation for one purpose or another. This can to some extent be verified in a less fictional manner by Pausanias who claimed that four pits were used in a rite to the winds where the priests muttered the incantations of Medea. Whereas the remaining *high* altars were all at public cult centres which were more concerned with religious activity than magickal works.

Therefore it is appropriate to build a high Olympian altar for personal (or group) devotional rites and other religious acts; and low Chthonic altars for acts of magick and summoning; this lends itself nicely towards personal shrines in a house being Olympian, however as it may well be impractical to physically dig a pit in your garden or back yard and it most certainly inappropriate to do so in a public place, when a *low* altar is necessary one constructed low to the ground will suffice.

1) Use the section on signs and symbols given in Appendix III to help you plan and build a devotional Olympian altar for Hekate.

2) Tend this shrine everyday for a month from new moon to new moon, write and recite prayers (some have been provided to get you started and can be found later in the book), light candles and take a short time every day to sit in front of the altar in reverence.

3) If possible also create a low altar either within your house or perhaps in your garden, there is precedent for this, for Medea claimed her central hearth was dedicated to Hekate and archaeologists have found deity figures below household fire-pits. If you can do this, from now on, perform all your acts of magick at this altar.

STATUARY

"Statues ensouled and conscious, filled with spirit and doing great deeds; statues that foreknow the future and predict by lots, by prophecy, by dreams and many other means"[18]

No self respecting shrine or temple, modern or ancient is complete without an effigy of the God or Goddess to whom it is dedicated; votive images of Hekate have been found and dated to as early as the 6th century BCE. The creation of these items was often the magnum opus of the creator showing great devotion to the deity involved. However in antiquity these statues and images were blessed and consecrated, cleaned, fumigated and anointed as part of the everyday ritual ablutions, the Gods and Goddesses literally resided within these carvings of wood and stone and each served a very specific purpose.

In modern times when reproductions of statuary and art work are so easily obtained, much of the mystery surrounding the creation, activation and attendance of such effigies has been forgotten. Without being disrespectful to certain deities, a certain demographic of the UK populace will understand totally the idea that current practitioners often have 'Athena' worship. For the rest of the world 'Athena' was a very popular franchise selling cheap poster copies of famous photographs and paintings, which were much favoured by pre-pubescent females and couples of the dual incomes but no kids yet demographic. They were put up, taken down and subsequently thrown away when they got tatty, tired and jaded. No reverence; no thought to the process of creation, and definitely no understanding of the inherent divinity that can be invited to reside within.

Installing a statue onto a shrine requires thought, ritual and most of all a request to the deity whose likeness it is supposed to represent to be in attendance, to actually make it ensouled and conscious. But the rite does not have to be elaborate, in ancient times as a sign of friendship, welcome and truce was to present a guest, welcome or otherwise with bread, salt and water, a gift that could not be refused and once taken ensured that the host family were treated with courtesy and respect. Your rite could simply be a request for the God or Goddess (in this case Hekate) to reside within the image, presenting her with the food items stated above, which can then be refreshed on a regular basis.

---

[18] Corpus Hermetica. Asclepius, C2nd-C3rd CE.

PRACTICAL EXERCISE: ENSOULING YOUR STATUE

Create or purchase an image that most depicts Hekate to you (remember this does not have to be a *'traditional'* image), consecrate the statue using the rite found below and then invite Hekate to reside in this image.

Consecration

> *"Give glory and honour and favour and fortune and power to this stone which I consecrate today"*[19]

The purpose of consecrating objects and space is to literally make them sacred, this concept was not unknown to the Greeks of ancient times, where animals were consecrated or *deified* through drowning and used in ritual, and items were often dedicated with the help of a deity. There are three very explicit examples of consecration in the *Greek Magical Papyri* and curiously all have a connection with Helios or the sun in another form; between them they give quite detailed instructions on how to set up an altar to consecrate an item, how to evoke the deity being called upon, what direction you should be oriented in and what libations should be used in this process; and it is this format we shall use in all our rites of consecration.

The Consecration of Hekate & Helios

As this is a magickal act, we will need to use a low chthonic altar in an easterly orientation using the following items:

- A clean altar cloth, preferably in either red, white, black or yellow
- Local flowers or greenery appropriate for the season
- Four candles, again preferably in red, white, black, or yellow
- The item you wish to consecrate
- A libation bowl or bowls containing any or all of the following, honey, milk, wine, olive oil.

Create a sacred space either using one of the circle techniques given in the section on sacred space, or alternatively one of your own. If you are choosing to consecrate your statue or magickal journal before you have learnt the circle casting techniques which are given shortly, then I would suggest that you just visualise a circle of bright blue flame surrounding both yourself and your working area.

Kneel (or sit if kneeling isn't possible) in front of the altar and raise both arms upwards using the gesture of praise (see section on *Ritual Gestures* for further explanation) then lower them to the ground and lightly touch the ground with your finger tips and keep them there for just a second; then clap your hands three times before lifting the object to be consecrated and holding it in both hands out before you, if possible on open palms as if in the sign of summoning.

Recite the following dedication inserting the name of object and purpose where appropriate, so for example a wand's purpose is to create sacred

---

[19] PGM IV:1596-1715, C2nd BCE – C5th CE.

space and to call forth the Gods to honour them and a journal is to record your journey with Hekate and so on.

> *"Come to me Helios and Hekate, you who are master and mistress above and below the earth, you who look to the west and the east and gaze upon the south and the north, world soul and ruler of the universe, together I evoke thee.*
>
> *Come and bestow your blessings upon this <<insert name of object>> which I consecrate in your honour for <<insert purpose of object>>."*

The item is now fit for use and should only be used for its stated purpose, should you wish to reuse it for another purpose then it would be best to cleanse it using a medium such as salt, running water or burying it for a period of time; then re-consecrating it to its new role.

PURIFICATION

Ritual purification of self and space played a huge part in both the cults and everyday lives of the ancient world. A lack of purity and preparedness was quite possibly the original sin, where sin is considered as an offense against a deity, rather than some set of rules which may or may not have appeared magickally to a Jewish mystic. These offenses were most often related to moral codes or taboos that may have had some long forgotten practical purpose but became entwined in religion, folklore and mythology.

Sometimes these codes appear to be almost conflicting, an excellent example, which relates well to our work with Hekate, is the possible taboos surrounding the Mysteries of Demeter and Persephone at Eleusis. Personally I believe that it wouldn't, considering the surviving mythologies, be too farfetched to assume that it would have been totally inappropriate to drink wine or consume pork prior to the rites of the Greater Mysteries; in fact the night before total abstinence was required. Now this may have had something to do with the ingredients of the Eucharistic drink Kykeon, which was consumed by all the initiates, but equally because the Goddess Demeter refused the offer of wine in the *Homeric Hymn to Demeter* and also because pigs were considered her sacred animal. Yet to gain the right to participate in the Greater Mysteries one first had to have undergone the lesser mysteries in the month of Anthesterion of the previous year which was undeniably connected to Dionysus the God of wine and to the ritual slaughter and consumption of pigs, so some taboos were often about context.

To understand it from a modern perspective there is a very good analogy to help us understand this without confusing it with the dogmas of today's established religions. Let us imagine we have been offered an interview for the job of our dreams paying vast sums of money and offering us both security and prestige, no sane person would consider turning up in old dirty crumpled clothes, reeking of curry and beer that had been consumed the night before now would they? And neither would you present an honoured guest in your home with a plate of rare beef and a glass of wine if they were vegetarian and teetotal, so why would anyone want to meet and welcome their Gods in a manner which could be deemed distasteful?

PERSONAL PREPARATION

> *"Asperges me domine, Purge me with Hyssop and I shall be clean, wash me and I shall be whiter than snow"*[20]

Personal preparation can be broadly separated into two categories, physical hygiene and appearance, and taboos and abstinence. For the latter, the *Greek Magical Papyri* is again an inspirational source and we shall address this in more detail shortly.

PHYSICAL HYGIENE AND APPEARANCE

Any form of personal purification should start with good old fashioned soap and water, yet this simple statement seems to have fallen on deaf ears when it comes to certain pagan and occult practitioners. To the Greeks the use of water in purification was one of the keystones of their purification practises, the washing of hands was well documented, and the witch Medea, an acolyte of Hekate herself, bathes seven times in running water before calling upon the Goddess.

Anybody wishing to undertake devotional or magickal work should at the very least wash their hands and face before entering sacred space, after all you can cleanse and banish your space until the cows come home but if you are dragging in a miasma of rubbish clinging to your person it is only going to be partially effective. This being said, just washing hands and face, whilst acceptable at a squeeze, is effectively perfunctory lip service to the act of ritual purification and completely misses much of the reason for performing what is, in itself, a powerful rite. So powerful is it that every person wishing to live a magickal and/or religious life should undertake it daily as part of their everyday practise. But why is it so powerful?

You've heard the saying *'washing your cares away'* right? Well therein lays one of the mysteries that are hidden in plain sight. When you roll over in bed in the morning and hug the pillow of your partner breathing in their perfume or aftershave a little bit of their aroma clings to you, later on the way to work as you sit on public transport next to the little old lady who looks not long for this world and smells of mothballs and fishermen's friend throat lozenges, a little bit of her clings to you too, you sit through a meeting at work and the boss's negative manner rubs off on you. So it goes on throughout the day, you slowly get grubbier and grubbier; a single smell, sound, sight or taste can evoke profound emotions for no apparent reason, the little lady hadn't made an obvious impact on your life but yet there you are thinking of her at 9 o' clock in the evening, your boss got taken out for lunch by a client and was his (or her) usual jolly self come mid afternoon yet you get home and grouch at your partner. You are quite literally physically and metaphysically filthy from your interactions of the day.

---

[20] Psalm 51, C10th-C2nd BCE.

Yet shedding your clothes and standing in the shower for a few minutes seem to lift you, it's not even just about physical cleanliness either, it can put you in a different headspace, those few minutes can allow you to process the things that need to be dealt with and to let the remainder disappear down the plug hole. And so it is with personal purification for magickal or religious purposes, not only are you presenting yourself in the best possible light in front of your Gods, but you are mentally shedding your mundane thoughts and actions in readiness for the work ahead.

Once bathed Medea instructed Jason to dress in dark robes prior to summoning the Goddess Hekate and indeed she herself dressed in special robes prior to performing her magickal rites and the idea of pure or clean clothes specifically for ritual was not uncommon. Many of the spells in the *Greek Magical Papyri* required the magician to dress in clean clothes, although it was often white linen rather than dark. Having special clothes for devotional and magickal rites is always a good idea, and this too is not just about appearance, it can be one of the first steps in making that mental shift between the mundane and the magick, putting on special clothes, pieces of ritual jewellery, brushing your hair (and it should be noted that the Thessalian witches summoned Hekate with unbound hair) can all be used as meditational devices that put you in the right frame of mind for the work ahead.

TABOOS AND ABSTINENCE

Taboos and abstinence were well accepted practices for the practitioner of magick and priests and priestesses of the Gods; sometimes the requirement was just for a few days, whilst for others such as the priestesses of Artemis for example, sexual abstinence was a lifelong vow.

There is no set formula for which taboos were required; many seem to be dependent on the specific deity and festival being celebrated or magickal operation being performed. Several types do occur more often than others within documents such as the *Greek Magical Papyri* and stand out because of their specific nature when many are so vague with the author or scribe just insisting that the magician performing the spell or magickal operation be pure; the length of time for abstinence also varies wildly for the examples listed below, but time frames of three and seven days seem to be the most usual.

For abstinence from animal foodstuffs, it is unclear if eggs and dairy would have been included in this as a number of papyri fragments specify the use and sometimes consumption of eggs as part of the operation. Pork is also mentioned on at least two occasions and is most probably the result of Jewish influences.

By uncooked foodstuffs, one has to assume this means fruit and vegetables rather than meat products although it is possible meat, milk, cheeses and eggs would also be included.

Wine falls into two categories, the former being a requirement for total abstinence, and the latter being the avoidance of wine that has not been diluted with seawater. The reason for this is as clear cut today as it was two thousand years ago, alcohol is a poison, it can affect judgement and even days later depending upon how heavily you drink, can affect reaction time, sleep, and general feelings of well being, however why it should be seawater is not specified.

Regarding abstinence from sexual intercourse, there is only one reference as to the specific type of intercourse, namely with a woman. The ancient Greeks were very open minded and as a result more openly homosexual than even perhaps occurs in modern society, in fact many believed that intercourse between men was more pure and of a higher nature than sexual intercourse with a woman, who was sometimes considered a lesser species to the male. Therefore it is possible that total abstinence was not always the norm as the author of the spell felt a need to specify what type of intercourse was inappropriate.

Considering sleeping in a bed, a good number of the fragments that list some form of preparatory rite mention the necessity of the magician to sleep on the floor or outside on matting prior to working the spell or performing the ritual, the purpose for this particular abstinence is unclear, perhaps poor sleep would make the magician more receptive to interactions with the Gods. Sleep deprivation has a well documented history for altering states of consciousness.

Refraining from speaking occurs on a few occasions, normally after one has risen from the makeshift bed that has been slept in the night prior to the spell or operation that is to be performed. One instance does insist on retiring to bed after the spell without speaking to another person, again the purpose for this is not given, however it would not be too farfetched to assume that this is to stop interaction with anybody who is not suitably pure and therefore capable of defiling the magician.

We can use the examples just as effectively now as our predecessors did millennia ago and although I feel no need to sleep on the floor I do ensure that I abstain from alcohol for a minimum of 24 hours before and I severely restrict my caffeine and meals are light and wherever possible context appropriate, for example a small plate of roasted Mediterranean vegetables, feta cheese and olives would be a very appropriate meal to consume before working with the Greek Gods, and one exception to my alcohol rule is Dionysus where I will happily consume a glass or two of wine (no more, remember: everything in moderation) and eat roasted pork for my meal prior to my work.

You will want to consider doing the same from here on in, after all it is all about ritual preparedness and non-offense to the entities and deities we wish to approach, and the foods, drinks and substances we consume and use can be just as fundamental a part of our ritual preparation as any other activity we may perform.

PURIFICATION OF RITUAL SPACE

"Cleansing the people of Miletus after a plague, by sprinkling them with water shaken from the leaves of a sacred laurel"[21]

Cleansing of ritual space by fumigation with incense and sprinkling with consecrated or sacred water have a long history; for example, the ancient Egyptians cleansed themselves and their ritual spaces by sprinkling with water and dressing their floor spaces with clean sand. The founder of the Oracle at Didyma was famous for curing the plague through acts of lustration (see quote under heading). Hekate has a very strong connection with purification of space and there were three very specific ritual purification acts associated directly with her, these were:

- Katharmarta - the leftovers not used in the ceremony, such as water or oil left in the libation jar.
- Katharsia - the remains of the offerings in ritual such as carcases of animals that were not burnt.
- Oxuthumia - left over incense and the dust and rubbish cleansed from the house and also the ritual site.

All of which were taken and left at the crossroads, from a spiritual and magickal perspective these activities are a necessary inclusion, for just as we would want to present ourselves in a state of ritual purity; it makes sense that the area in which we call the Goddess should also be clean and prepared.

Historically it would also have had a very practical purpose, as it ensured that rotting food and vegetation is not left to cause a health hazard within the temple environs or the home, and although we don't throw our leftovers onto the floor anymore, a good session of housework can leave the whole atmosphere of a home markedly different. It of course goes without saying that we should not be cleaning our house and dumping our detritus all over the nearest road, if for no other reason than fly tipping and littering impose quite hefty fines, but there are things that can be done in the spirit of this practise.

PRACTICAL EXERCISE – RITUAL CLEANSING OF SPACE

As part of your regular devotional work you should tend to the cleanliness of your shrine if you already have one, if not wait until you have covered this later in the book. Tasks could include washing the altar cloth, dusting any statuary, removing decaying offerings and refreshing them with new. Set aside a time once a month, before the new moon to do this. Flowers and other organic materials can be composted and it would be a nice touch to hand wash the altar cloth, that way a small vial of the waste water along with a pinch of dust from the vacuum cleaner can be taken out and deposited at a crossroads without fear of reprisal.

---

[21] Ancient Greek Divination, Johnston, 2008.

Leftovers from rituals and devotional offerings are a little more tricky, should you have the luxury of an open fire, chimenea or fire bowl then it would be appropriate to burn them, if that isn't possible again I would advise that the majority of the cleansings be disposed of in a responsible and appropriate manner. Food stuffs such as fruit and even meat, should you use any, could be left for the wildlife in your back yard, but do beware, this could attract rats and whilst rats themselves are not dirty creatures, sadly due to living in human sewage they can carry Weil's disease so are not desirable neighbours. Again a token offering could be left in an appropriate place, at the end of the day, common sense should prevail and it is the thought that counts not necessarily the quantity.

ENERGETIC PURIFICATION

In many magickal and spiritual traditions both western and eastern alike there is, quite rightly, a strong emphasis on energetic work, although in recent times, the purpose of these practices has been omitted, often leaving the practitioner wondering the age old question of *Why?*

This omission may well be because so much has previously been written by eminent occultists over the years on the subject, that it is now considered to be taken as read, that anybody walking the path of magick and interaction with the divine, will already be aware of the fundamental role energetic work plays in travelling that path and whilst ideally this should be true, in practise this is often not the case.

Energetic work serves a multitude of purposes, in the early days of practise it is fundamental to teaching discipline, control, and can even help balance and harmonise the body and spirit through a connection with the divine energies that permeate this universe. As a person advances it can be used to focus one's will and project energy into healing, the production of talismans, facilitate the assumption of Godforms in ritual (the ritualistic act of identification with and awakening of aspects of a particular deity) and even direct and create tangible communion with the divine essence a person might wish to either evoke or even invoke.

It can also be used as an excellent medium for effectively purifying the spirit and mind in preparation for any ritual work to be undertaken. It's all well and good to have cleansed your body and sacred space physically but if your heart and mind is still a quagmire of thoughts and emotions and far from focused on the task ahead, you are not in the state of being ritually prepared, you are in effect unclean.

Many modern traditions have focused on the eastern techniques of yoga and working with the chakras and this is all well and good, and although over time much of the teaching has become watered down, it is still a valid balancing and centring exercise for those that choose to devote time, practise and patience in mastering the techniques involved. However, evidence of these practices being used, despite the possible links with Indian trade routes during the Hellenic and Imperial eras, is negligible.

PRACTICAL EXERCISE – THE TETRAHEDRON

The following exercise was transcribed during a rite of balancing and rebirth, in which Hekate was evoked. It was subsequently explored and practised by two of the participants over the period of one lunar month. The results were very interesting and both people received different things from performing this exercise on a daily basis, however it was agreed that each felt energetically more balanced and in control. The priestess in question previously had no knowledge of the *Greek Magical Papyri* so it was also surprising to note that the gestures used bore some notable similarity to the ritual of the heptagram which was considered a *'spell to which the God gives attention.'*[22]

Imagine a tetrahedron, one of the purest geometric forms. It is known as a platonic solid and occultists, religious practitioners and scientists alike have been trying to attribute the meaning of life, the universe and everything, to these fundamental shapes for time immemorial. Whilst the tetrahedron is traditionally attributed to the element of fire, it can be used as a representation of all the elements combined in harmony and it is this aspect of the shape that we shall be using in the following exercise.

You will need to be able to visualise yourself sitting within the tetrahedron, and if you gain nothing else from this exercise it will help you practise this skill which will come in handy later on when things become a little more complex. The rite as it was transmitted, was designed to be performed at either dawn or dusk and no protective circle or sacred space was created, as it was felt that being *enclosed* within the tetrahedron itself was sufficient; if however you feel moved to create a protective or sacred space prior to this, go ahead, intuition is a very useful skill that should be encouraged rather than ignored. Details of possible circle techniques can be found in the next section.

Each ritual gesture is intended to be held for at least three minutes, however you will find very quickly in the early days that this is something that comes with practise, so do not stress too much if initially you find this impossible. It will also mean that you will need sufficient time undisturbed to perform this exercise.

Light candles, dim light, seat yourself comfortably as appropriate, it is preferable to sit cross legged on the floor but use your common sense to adapt this if it isn't possible.

---

[22] PGM XIII:734-1077, C2nd BCE – C5th CE.

HEYAT

This is a position of stillness, try and clear your mind and breathe deeply and listen for your heart beat.

HANDS

Left – Palm up to the point of the tetrahedron.

Right – Palm to heart.

KEPFIA

This is the element of air, and its colour is yellow/orange.

HANDS

Left – Palm flat on the side of the tetrahedron.

Right – Fingertips on 3rd eye.

APALON

This is the element of water, and its colour is silver/light blue.

HANDS

Left – Palm to the womb/stomach.

Right – Palm flat on the side of the tetrahedron.

MAPET

This is the element of earth, and its colour is green.

HANDS

Left – Fingertips over mouth.

Right – Flat to the front of the tetrahedron.

HADIA

This is the element of fire, and its colour is red.

HANDS

Should be crossed right over left and palms touching the floor, your head should also be bowed down.

APREA

This again returns you to a state of calm and stillness, and is the end of the exercise.

HANDS

Left – Back of hand pressed to heart palm out.

Right – Palm up to the top of the tetrahedron.

Write up any experiences you have whilst performing this exercise, consider the following:

- Sounds and words.
- Sensations both internally and externally.
- Smells.
- Entities or even animals you may have encountered.
- Initially try to complete this exercise every day for at least a week which should help you memorise the gestures; after that it is a valuable tool to use as part of your ritual preparations.

MAKING A ROBE

Having a special item of clothing in which to perform ritual can add an extra layer of separation from the mundane world, also when working in a group, a uniform manner of dressing can also help develop a group identity. It is possible to buy many wonderful items of ritual clothing online and through local occult stores. However, making your own robes can be a magickal act that makes the final item even more special.

Luckily for us, due to their simplicity, traditional Greek style clothing of the Classical and Hellenic eras is reproducible with little knowledge of dressmaking and needle work; and depending upon the style of robe you choose to make, you do not even need to use a sewing machine if you do not wish for both techniques yield comparable results.

THE DORIC ROBE (CHITON)

This type of robe was worn by both men and women; the female version was floor length; whilst the men's version was normally knee length.

This style of robe was normally of wool and was constructed using one piece of material that was wrapped around the body and fastened at the shoulder and around the waist.

This style of gown predated the Ionic chiton, and was in later years considered a rustic or provincial item of clothing.

1) Take a length of fabric which is 6-8 inches (15-20cm) wider than the desired robe length, and long enough to wrap around your body with a reasonable overlap. (a)

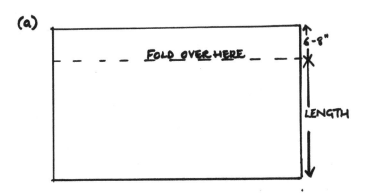

2) Fold Over the top 6-8 inches (15-20cm), using an iron to make a crease will help this fold stay in place whilst you wrap the robe around you. (b)

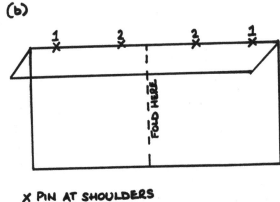

X PIN AT SHOULDERS

3) Fold the fabric in half around your body, and pin at the shoulders, use a cord or ribbon to tie the robe shut. (c)

THE IONIC ROBE

Again worn by both genders as described above, this chiton was constructed from two pieces of material sewn together.

This style was often of linen and used more material to create artistic folds and drapes, although it still normally fastened at the shoulder and around the waist.

They tended to be more heavily adorned with patterns and sometimes dyed with natural colours.

1) Take two identical rectangular pieces of fabric again 6-8 inches (15-20cm) longer than your desired length and wide enough to fit comfortably around the widest part of your body. (a)

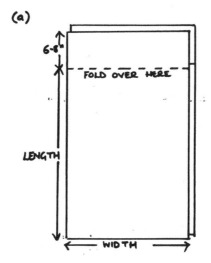

2) Sew the two pieces of fabric together along 50% of the lengths of the fabric, creating a partial tube, then hem the bottom of the tube. (b)

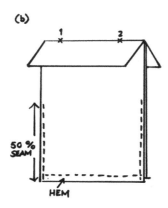

X PIN AT SHOULDERS

3) Turn the tube so the hems face inwards and again pin the robe at the shoulders on the open end of the fabric tube and tie with cord or ribbon.(see diagram c above)

As an interesting side note, the wheel motif we so often see associated with Hekate, most probably derives from a design taken from a Mycenaean button used to attach clothing and it unlikely to have any ancient spiritual meaning, however to include it as a design element in your ritual attire would be especially appropriate; you may even like to fashion brooches from clay or another modelling medium using this design for fastening your robes.

If you really do feel that making your ritual attire is beyond your capabilities it is perfectly fine to purchase a robe or even choose something special from your wardrobe, wash and iron it and then consecrate it for ritual use with the ritual provided in the section on consecration.

From now prior to ritual take time to dress and prepare for the task ahead, make it part of the ritual itself, you may even want to choose items of jewellery and even specific perfumes or aftershaves which are worn only during your devotional and magickal rites; the first few times you do this write about how this makes you feel and if you felt it had an effect on the rite itself.

RITUAL GESTURES

"If, however, he comes close to you, take hold of your right heel and recite the following".[23]

Religion and magick the world over is, from a certain perspective a ritual dance, Crowley[24] admits as much and wrote at reasonable length on the importance of gesture within ritual. This wasn't a whim on his part in an attempt to validate his own desire for drama, as he observed, the practitioners of Shinto clap their hands together four times to banish evil spirits.

The ancient Egyptians were also aware of the sacred dance and the power of movement, the *Pyramid Texts* and *Coffin Texts* are littered with hieroglyphs of bodily gestures representing such concepts as praise, invocation, devotion, protection and summoning. These movements it seems either through cross-pollination or through independent evolution appear to have also existed in the rituals of Ancient Greece. Medea and Kirke naturally raise their arms to heaven when petitioning Hekate for help and a seal shows Zeus holding Hekate in his outstretched palm as if in the Egyptian pose of summoning.

The combinations and types of gesture do vary fairly wildly but there is a sufficient number that correlate sufficiently enough for us to comment upon and use within our own rites.

Gesture	Purpose
Pointing	Protective / Cursing
Holding Thumbs	Apotropaic
Holding Heels	Apotropaic
Praise	Adoration / Veneration/ Evocation
Summoning	Evocation
Vision	Divination / Invocation

Obviously some of these gestures will require practise for you to use them fluidly and with confidence, the diagrams below depict each of the gestures and are accompanied with a textual description for clarification.

---

[23] Greek Magical Papyri, Betz, 1992.
[24] Book 4, Crowley, 1998.

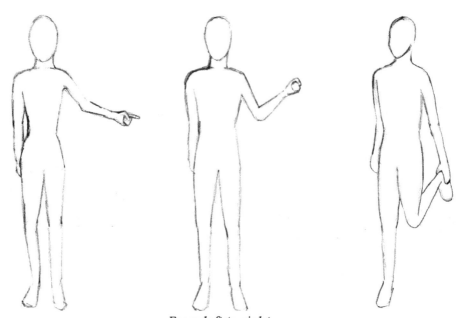

From left to right
Pointing, Holding Thumbs, Holding Heels

- Pointing - A fist clenched pointing with thumb and forefinger, a bit like when you were a child firing an imaginary gun.

- Holding thumbs – A fist clenched with the thumb enclosed in the fist.

- Holding Heels – Stood on one foot, leg tucked up behind, corresponding arm holding the heel to the buttock.

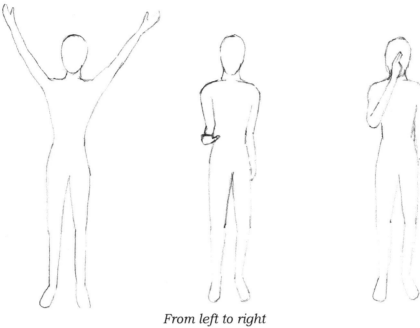

From left to right
Praise, Summoning, Vision

- Praise – Stood with arms raised above head, palms upwards.

- Summoning – Stood left hand by the side, right arm extended outwards in front of you palm upwards, like someone holding their hand out to receive something.

- Vision – Pressing first and second finger of right hand against third eye.

PRACTICAL EXERCISE

Practise these movements regularly until you feel confident performing each one, as you progress through the book try incorporating them into rites of divination, evocation and protection.

Meditate on each of the gestures and make notes regarding any thoughts, images, sounds or smells that present themselves to you; write these down and consider using them as part of your magickal rites.

SACRED VOWELS

"When these seven heavens sing together they produce a perfect harmony which ascends as an everlasting praise to the throne of the Creator."[25]

Along with movement, sound also played an important part in the rituals of the ancient world, Pythagoras was fascinated with the connection between music and the universe and others believed that each of the sacred vowels were assigned to a planetary body.

Many of the charms in the *Greek Magical Papyri* spells contain sounds such as hissing and popping, barbarous names, and also the seven (sacred) vowels of the Greek Alphabet. Scholars have dedicated whole life times to the study of these sounds and words and to cover it in depth would require a book all of its own. However the chanting of the sacred vowels can be, without doubt, one of the most effective evocatory devices you can ever employ. It is particularly suited for group work, where different people chant different vowels over and over again to a point of climax. What starts initially as a cacophony of sound, does as the quote above suggest eventually transform into the most mind blowing harmony you can ever experience, its clarity can only be likened to an Angelic choir.

The vowels and their names are included in a table below, along with the planet they are most commonly associated with and a pronunciation guide.

Vowel	Symbol	Pronunciation	Planet
Alpha	A	"A" as in "at"	Moon
Epsilon	E	"Eh" as in "set"	Mercury
Eta	H	"Air" as in "pair"	Venus
Iota	I	"Ih" as in "it"	Sun
Omicron	O	"Oh" as in "spot"	Mars
Upsilon	Y	"Ooo" as in "blue"	Jupiter
Omega	Ω	"O" as in "flow"	Saturn

PRACTICAL EXERCISE

Use the vowel sounds like a mantra chanting them repeatedly, note how it makes you feel; then over a period of days, try just using one vowel at a time, again note down your thoughts and feelings.

---

[25] Against Heresies, Iraneus, C2nd CE.

If working with a group try group chanting with different individuals chanting different vowels, how did this make the group feel, what were the harmonic results, if any?

Incenses can also be made and empowered with the use of chanting and a number of Hekate specific recipes are listed in the next section, one is also included for use in rituals where using the Sacred Vowels and chanting whilst pounding and mixing this blend is particularly appropriate.

INCENSE

"They burn incense of myrrh; for its heat loosens and disintegrates the turbid and muddy mass which gathers in the atmosphere"[26]

Our sense of smell is probably one of the most powerful evocatory tools we have, a single aroma can conjure up images and memories vividly; and assail our emotions so strongly that it can move us to tears or laughter. The mix of a rich tobacco and the slightly sickly scent of decaying roses might transport us back thirty years, transforming us once again to the small child who wandered adoringly round the garden with a beloved grandfather inspecting the plants, or the whiff of watery cabbage returning us to our school days, dinner queues and wet play times.

And these images, when accompanied by a smell are often exquisitely detailed far more detailed than if you tried to conjure up the image alone. Cultures in times gone by were more than aware of this phenomena, and as a result used incense for purification, adoration and evocation to name but a few. The Egyptians believed that the perfumes created from certain plants and resins originated from the bodies of the Gods themselves and therefore burning them was a sympathetic means of connecting with the God themselves.

The Greeks were also fond of this means of conversing with their Gods, when Simaetha burnt the bay leaves whilst cursing her inconsiderate lover, it would not have just been because of the magickal properties of the bay itself, but for the aroma and the connection with the Goddess she was evoking to aid her in her task. They too often named herbs after deities, they were particularly fond of these being bodily secretions, for example, wormwood was considered the blood of Hephaestus, and white hellebore the semen of Helios and aconite as we know sprang from the saliva of Kerberus the hound of Hades.

Mixing and burning our own incenses can enrich and enliven our rites, the time taken to prepare the ingredients, harvesting them if you are lucky enough to have the space and the green fingers to grow them yourself, mixing them according to planetary hours and purpose can all add an extra layer to the magick we work. Below are some basic recipes which are suitable for use within different rites to Hekate, but feel free to experiment and create your own.

---

[26] Isis and Osiris, Plutarch, C1st CE

HOW TO MAKE AND BURN YOUR OWN

Equipment Needed

A Pestle and Mortar (or for the really lazy an electric herb chopper but make sure it's kept solely for this purpose) - granite or ceramic pestle and mortars are preferable to wooden ones especially if working with harder woods and resins or particularly strong herbs and oils.

Measuring spoons, the chrome sets found in supermarkets are ideal and normally not particularly expensive.

Air tight containers, some herbs don't react too well to light, so if possible try and get some brown glass jars; they can be purchased in bulk from a number of online stores.

Incense, pestle & mortar and spoons

To Burn Loose Incense

- Incense
- Self igniting charcoal disks
- Heat resistant dish or censer (avoid flat Pyrex candle holders, they might take the heat of candle burning low but it will explode once the disk reaches full temperature)

Procedure for burning the Incense

Light the charcoal block with a lighter, some brands of charcoal are more temperamental than others so matches often don't burn long enough for them to take, one of the long nosed candle lighters is a good option as your hand will be far enough away from the flame that you won't suddenly be yelping with a burnt thumb as the lighter heats up. You will see red sparks spread across the charcoal as it takes and it is at this point you want to place it into the heat proof container.

Let it sit for a while and wait until it glows red hot, this has the added benefit of allowing the remaining accelerant that is impregnated into the charcoal to burn off so your incense won't initially be tainted with a chemical smell.

Add the loose grains, a quarter of a teaspoon at a time is normally sufficient, little mustard spoons are ideal for this purpose and very ornate ones can be found in charity shops and flea-markets making them a nice addition to your altar paraphernalia. Don't be tempted to overdo it for a number of reasons; smoke can irritate, especially if you have any kind of respiratory disorder and excessive smoke can be downright unpleasant, also many incenses smell delightful in small quantities but become intolerably overpowering in excess, watering eyes, tickly throats and stinking like a bonfire is a sure fire way of ruining the magick of any ritual, be assured of that.

General Altar Incense

An adaptation of a recipe from Late Antiquity,[27] it should be burnt very sparingly. It is suitable for general full and dark moon rituals.

Take equal parts of:

- Frankincense
- Bay
- Myrrh
- Rue
- Storax

Four Elements Incense[28]

Blend all the ingredients together and burn, the basic incense is suitable for use during the four elemental meditations. Should you wish to use a

---

[27] Witchcraft Medicine, Mueller-Ebeling et al., 2003.

[28] Adapted from Hekate of Heaven, Earth & Underworld Incense, Hekate Keys to the Crossroads, d'Este (ed), 2006.

generic incense rather than the perfumes specified, an additional 6 Bay leaves, 1 tbsp of Mugwort and 1 tbsp of Sandalwood can be added to the ingredients above to make very good incense for trance work and divination, but again use very sparingly in a well ventilated area.

- 4 tbsp Frankincense
- 1 tbsp Myrrh
- 2 tbsp Dried Mugwort
- 2 tsp Cinnamon powder
- 2 tbsp Lavender flowers
- 4 drops Cypress oil

Seven Planets and Sacred Vowels Incense

Whilst not specifically a Hekate Incense, it does contain many herbs and resins appropriate for use when working with Hekate, particularly if your work is also of a planetary nature. It is very similar in smell to the four elements incense just a little sweeter and less woody. It is also useful incense for rituals involving the seven planets or the Sacred Vowels, for information both the planet and the vowel is written in brackets beside the ingredient.

- 3 tbsp Frankincense (Sun - Iota)
- 1 tbsp Myrrh (Moon - Alpha)
- 2 tbsp Dried Mugwort (Venus - Eta)
- ½ tsp Dragons Blood (Mars - Omicron)
- 2 tbsp Lavender flowers (Mercury - Epsilon)
- 8 drops Cypress oil (Saturn - Omega)
- 2 tbsp of Hyssop (Jupiter - Upsilon)

He-kyphi

Kyphi is ancient Egyptian temple incense, which also had certain medical applications. It is mentioned a number of times in the *Greek Magical Papyri*; several other kyphi style incenses which were rolled into small pellets and burnt were also used, some in conjunction with rituals related to Hekate. The quantities given here are rather large and as a result the incense will, unless you live in a very warm country, take months to dry to a consistency where it can be rolled if you add all the ingredients at once, so you may wish to grind the raisins, dried ingredients and resins together first and then *feed* the wine in slowly and finally add the honey last. However, allowing it to dry for such a long time develops the smell considerably, if burnt before the incense has had chance to mature, it smells very sweet and is very smoky, but later it is a very delicate fragrance with minimal smoking if used just one pellet at a time.

This particular recipe is an adaptation of one given by the Greek medical practitioner Dioscordes, but has been adapted to contain herbs and resins that more closely align to Hekate, it is suitable for use at dark moon rituals and temple rituals invoking or evoking Hekate herself.

- 1400g Raisins (try and obtain ones that have not been oiled to make them shine)
- 2 Pints of Mavrodaphne (or other rich sweet red wine, port is also a possibility)
- 250g Honey
- 100g Frankincense
- 50g Myrrh
- 40g Cinnamon
- 35g Juniper
- 15g Cardamom
- 10g Cumin
- 5g Lemon Grass
- 1g Saffron
- 1 tsp Storax

Note: Once dried and rolled this is best stored in an airtight container, but not before as it could make the ingredients go mouldy.

BANISHING RITUAL

Many of the best known banishing rituals, have their roots firmly planted in ceremonial traditions, such as the Golden Dawn; they are one of many *'high magick'* techniques that have crossed the boundaries into other modern traditions, possibly because of their simplicity and effectiveness. But banishing malevolent spirits is not a new concept by any stretch of the imagination banishing or evil averting rituals and spells are found regularly in antiquity across a broad range of cultures, fear of spirits who could cause harm seems to have been fairly pandemic.

Within a formal learning environment it is often one of the very first things a neophyte has to master, and it often practised two to three times a day for many months, and with good reason, if you aren't capable of clearing up your own mess then you really have no place creating one in the first place.

Performing a banishing both prior to and after ritual can help clear your immediate vicinity of negative energies and unsolicited entities, and regular practise can also help balance both body and to some extent the mind, after all, negative energies aren't always external.

The following ritual itself takes only a few minutes to complete and once mastered on the physical realms is just as effective on the astral which is why it can be used to clear the astral space around you if you encounter an entity which you wish to be rid of either before progressing further on your astral journey, working in your astral temple or even returning to your physical form.

THE EYES OF HEAVEN

1) Stand facing east and raise your arms in the gesture of praise.

2) **Say:**

   Hail to thee Helios the Lord most high, and Hail Queen Hekate of the Infernal realms. I summon you forth both night and day, light and darkness, for I am your Priest/ess and I carry the eyes of heaven in my hands. For I am the bearer of the immortal flame and my heart is encircled with serpents.

3) Take one step forward towards the east and hold out your arms whilst performing the gesture of the holding of thumbs, stamp your foot once.

4) **Say:**

> Go forth from this place lest the eyes of heaven seek you out and consume you, Helios from the uprising and the down going and Hekate in heaven and hell, else be bound and banished in fetters indestructible and cast down nine days hence to the realms of Tartarus.

5) Release your thumbs and move around to face South, West, and North, each time repeating the holding of thumbs and stamping the ground, each time also repeating 4) above.

6) Once you have returned to the East, kneel and strike the ground 3 times with the flat of your hand.

7) **Say:**

> Earth gape, maw of Tartarus yawn, By Hekate your infernal Queen, and by the Chariot of Helios that nightly travels through your realm; Eyes of Heaven receive this noisome spirit into perdition and subject them to my will so that they become obedient to my wishes and commands and hence forth shall bother me no more.

CREATING SACRED SPACE

WHAT IS SACRED SPACE?

Some places are inherently sacred, whether that is because in millennia gone by, some long forgotten tribe marked the space for a deity or celebration and somehow the energy imparted in that space has remained, perhaps a little different or jaded, but there none the less. Other spaces are only sacred to a particular person or group, to the rest of the world, it may just be a nice green area, a dark murky cave, or a barren hillside; but something affected that person or group using that space and made them catch their breath, a feeling of awe and rightness filling them.

But why do we find these places so special and what do we do when we have need of a sacred space and none is immediately present?

In essence a sacred space is one that is apparently removed from the mundane world. It is a place that is closer to *the other*, something that is not of this world, call it supernatural, deity or whatever you will. It is a place where you feel that God/dess is listening and will communicate with you. It is also a place of safety, where the unknown, and even the known but undesirable, cannot harm you. When you happen across these spaces in the world, these pockets of space where the other coexists more closely with the mundane, it can be a very profound experience.

Not everyone will sense these pockets the same, this often has to do with personal theologies and worldviews. Some will tell you that they can only exist in nature, and that to truly interact with the otherworld you must find some wooded grove, stream, hillside etc. that is imbued with mystical power. And of course you will find these places. Sadly for the majority of magickal practitioners living in this thoroughly modern world, the closest thing many perceive as achievable on a regular basis is a walk in the park, which can lead to intense frustration.

In reality sacred space is wherever we choose to make it; we can facilitate that thinning so that the sacred and the mundane can be coincident. Sit down on a public bench on a busy street on a warm summer's evening, just sit and feel the energy that the daily commuters create, go to an old cotton mill and place your ear on the brick work and listen to the energy of the place, you may be surprised as quite how sacred these industrialised, manmade, places really feel. There is a lot of evidence to suggest that Hekate was a very domestic Goddess, she stood as guard between here and there, between the sacred and the mundane. She was found as often in urban situations as on the barren crossroads. She can be accessed in both the field and the city.

And just as we can facilitate making a specific place permanently sacred by altering our perceptions of a place, we can create these pockets of the sacred at will and disperse them just as readily. A magick circle is a well established medium with which to accomplish this task and far from being a modern construct there is some evidence that the magick circle may be as many as 4500 years old. In some cultures the use of a sacred or magick circle was incorporated if the rite was one that may involve necromancy or evocation of a spirit of a demonic nature, the thinning between sacred and mundane and the raw power that can be accessed and if raised, then subsequently contained, not only helped amplify the calling forth but also tapped into the protective power of the divine.

Many readers will have already learnt a specific method for circle casting and in this instance there is absolutely no reason why you should deviate from this, others will have read any number of books with a million different permutations of the ritual circle and if there is one that particularly strikes you as meaningful then go ahead and use this. Remember this isn't a book of dogma, it is one person's perspective and this one person actively encourages growth and adaptation where appropriate. The point is that a space be created, the actual mode is almost irrelevant, if a square or a triangle means more to you then try it and see what happens; of course the examples given below may then have little meaning and therefore if you are planning to use an alternative geometric construction, some careful thought on your part will be required and careful assessment made as to the suitability of your adaptation. The circle has a long and successful history and you may have to ask yourself, *"If it isn't broke, why fix it"?* But for those of you that have not used a circle before, or would like to try a different version, the following examples have been created by drawing upon historical texts.

BASIC CIRCLE STRUCTURE

> *"Then Eastward twice and Westward twice she turned, Thrice sang a spell, Thrice touched him with her wand"*[29]

Most magick circles used by modern witches and magicians and the tools and symbols used to construct them, are often based upon the instructions given in the *Key of Solomon*, sometimes with a few minor differences which are also discussed although only briefly below, after all, other authors have already conducted in depth studies of this phenomena and the interested reader might like to consider researching this in more detail themselves using the resources given in the bibliography.

<u>Size of the Circle</u> – In many modern magical traditions the circle is normally described as nine feet in diameter; this size is more than sufficient for any individual to practise their magickal arts and is at a squeeze adequate for group ceremonies. This is a size that can normally be achieved in even the most space poor accommodations where a living area may have to also double as a ritual space; however, the internal circle in the *Key of*

---

[29] Metamorphoses XIV 387-388, Ovid, 8 CE.

Solomon was in fact nine feet in radius (not diameter);[30] so for the purpose of the rituals in this work, assume that the circle is nine foot in diameter but if space allows or working outdoors, you may like to consider increasing the size of the circle to match the original Solomonic circle, it certainly facilitates more free movement during group ritual.

Marking the Circle - The *Key of Solomon* describes the marking of a further two circles emanating outwards from the middle circle, each one foot apart resulting in three concentric circles. Within these circles were marked certain hexagrams, symbols and God names in Hebrew, but over time this has been done away with in a lot of modern pagan practise so that only one circle remains, which may or may not be marked physically on the floor. If at all possible, try and mark out the circle physically, using flour, chalk, petals, ribbon or rope; obviously common sense should prevail, don't go ruining a perfectly good fitted carpet by attempting to roll it back or grinding in tonnes of flour and if working outdoors, make sure whatever you use is non-toxic, bio-degradable, safe for consumption by any indigenous wildlife and/or easily removed from the site upon departure. The foil dregs of tea-lights are no offering to the Gods, be assured of that.

The Altar – Most modern circle constructions include an altar which is normally either positioned at the northern quarter or placed in the centre of the circle oriented such that to work at the altar facilitates a north facing position; apologies to people in the southern hemisphere that have a deep desire to turn things upside down, but Hekate most probably originated north of the equator, there is little benefit in trying to reverse things, work with her isn't primarily agricultural and the north pole is still, well, north basically.

There are two distinct types of altar to be considered, one that is generally more appropriate to Hekate than the other is the chthonic altar, unless otherwise stated, it is preferable that your altar be of a chthonic style, either dug into the ground if possible or constructed low to the floor, if you are working indoors try and include some form of receptacle in which oil, water and wine offerings can be poured, as they are a nightmare to get out of cloths and carpet. Orientation of the altar is a matter of personal preference, and you may choose to orient it according to a tradition in which you already work, if you are unsure then it might be best to stick to North or centre as given in the examples below.

Tools Required – Both in the *Key of Solomon* and now in neo-pagan circles it is most common to cast a circle with a black handled knife or a sword, however there is a precedent also for a wand to be used and many modern ritual magicians consecrate both their wands and knives to both fire and air, which is most likely as a result of older practises. Considering the use of the protective *branch* in rites of summoning in the *Greek Magical Papyri* (which we will discuss in the later section on sacred objects); and Ovid who as we also know had Kirke perform her magick rites with the aid of

---

[30] The Veritable Key of Solomon, Skinner & Rankine, 2008:363.

a wand, it is therefore more appropriate for a wand to be used in the circle casting process, and unless otherwise stated it should be taken as read that a wand is used for this purpose when a circle is required in the rites given later on.

Direction of Casting – Modern neo-pagan magickal practise tends to also work in a clockwise direction for invocations and evocations and anticlockwise for banishing, which may show an influence from the works of Crowley, although some neo-pagans now refuse to work anticlockwise or *widdershins* perceiving it to be sinister or malevolent, which is a little misguided, but understandable. This being said, a few of the papyri rituals required the operator to face the sunrise, effectively starting the operation facing east, and on a number of occasions although not explicitly stated it appears the operator of the spell had to address the sun at different hours of the day creating at least a partial circle in a deosil or sun-wise manner. Completely circular perambulations were also not unheard of, in one case it occurs in the form of a trench that has to be dug entirely around an altar and in another it involves salutations to the directions, again in a deosil direction; therefore the circle castings in the rites given should move deosil.

Consecration and Purification – The consecration and purification of space has an established history across a number of cultures, even to this present day. How this is performed in modern pagan and magickal practise is often tradition dependant. But as there is such a precedent for cleansing and purification rites which are connected with Hekate, it would be remiss not to include these important actions as part of the circle construction, therefore the circle should be both fumigated with incense and sprinkled with consecrated water.

PREPARING THE CIRCLE AREA

Below are two examples of circle construction, they are prepared similarly and serve the same purpose, protection and sacred space.

As the entire purpose of creating sacred space is so that we may work with and for Hekate, the first stage of the preparation process should be a cleansing or Oxuthumia. If you can get hold of a dust-buster, manual carpet sweeper or small Hoover that can be kept solely for this purpose then do so, although a household dustpan and brush will suffice, as the dust collected should either be added to the ritual incense to be burnt, or taken out with the offerings and disposed of appropriately once the ritual is complete.

Next you need to physically mark the circle, in flour or chalk or even with rope or ribbon. Some dedicated souls have large sheets or pieces of lino with the circle and any appropriate sigils, God names, Hebrew letters etc. pre-marked, so that all is required is to lay it down like a rug prior to the physical acts required to activate the circle, and it can be lifted again and stored away at the end of the rite. If you have good visualisation skills this of course is not necessary, many witches for example pride themselves that the only tool that they need is their index finger. However, most of the rituals given later do assume that, unless you are working in a dedicated temple space, some form of formally constructed circle is present so bear that in mind.

Candles and/or ritual objects should be placed at the quarters, in the case of the first circle example these ritual objects relate to the entities being called to stand guardian at the circle perimeter and have been listed below. However, these objects normally in modern practise have some form of elemental attributions associated with them, such as incense for air, a candle for fire, a bowl of liquid for water and sand or salt for earth, and this is the case for the second circle example given. Which direction those elements are assigned to will also be tradition dependant so some discretion and common sense must be used, especially if you wish to adapt the circles given below. As time goes on and as you work further through the exercises in the book you may also want to deviate away from standard elemental attributions, but make sure you totally understand why you are doing this and approach with caution.

In the first example, two altars should be erected in the centre of the circle, an Olympian high altar for the father of the winds Astraios (description given below) and directly below a Chthonic altar to the Goddess Hekate. In the second example only a chthonic altar to Hekate is required. In both cases the Hekate altar should be dressed with appropriate symbolism depending upon the purpose of the rite and the aspect of Hekate you are working with.

All of the above should be considered as much part of the ritual as the actual ritual itself and should be conducted with the appropriate demeanour. Ritual preparations are very important for adopting the correct state of mind and preparedness, this does not necessarily mean that all ritual preparation should be a grim and solemn affair; rites of celebration should have an appropriately jovial atmosphere. The point is to be mindful of the work that is about to commence and to tune into the correct energy currents as part of the preparation.

CASTING THE CIRCLE – EXAMPLE 1

> *"There is an altar of winds, where the priest sacrifices to the winds on one night of every year. He performs other rites which are not to be spoken of, using four pits taming the savagery of the air, and in fact they say he sings the incantations of Medea"*[31]

The justification for using the winds as elemental guardians in relation to Hekate is very specific and comes from the excerpt quoted above, Pausanias describes a sacred space adjacent to the Temple of Athena in Titane, which is in the region of Corinth; and whilst more modern translations omit a connection to Hekate, preferring to state that the rites performed could not be spoken of, earlier translations say that these rites were *'of Hekate'*, but even without this vague translation connection, what is

---

[31] Description of Greece Book II, Pausanias, C2nd CE.

clear is that the rites performed there involved incantations of Medea, who is a well documented Priestess of Hekate.

THE ALTAR TO ASTRAIOS

Astraios, also sometimes syncretised with the Roman God Aeolus is; depending upon which mythology you study, either king or father of the winds. He is sometimes, like Hekate, considered a Titan God and according to Nonnus a great seer and prophet, who predicted the abduction of Persephone, a story in which we already know Hekate plays a pivotal part. But although he is considered Titan, he is not Chthonic therefore it is appropriate that his altar is a *high* Olympian altar.

> *"Old Astraios heard it and arose; he had covered the surface of a table with dark dust, where he was describing in traced lines a circle with the tooth of his rounding tool, within which he inscribed a square in the dark ashes, and another figure with three equal sides and angles."*[32]

This altar should be placed in the centre of the circle and can be decorated simply with the image of a triangle which in turn resides within a square. However, should you wish to be more elaborate then decorate it with equestrian imagery, for one of his titles was Aeolus Hippotades, which can be roughly translated as *'Aeolus who reins the horses.'* This is because the four winds that were either his sons or his charges were often depicted as horse shaped spirits. Astraios was also God of the stars and in some mythologies the father of Perses, who is considered Hekate's father, this effectively would make Astraios Hekate's grandfather which makes his inclusion in the circle construction even more fitting. Other appropriate items might be stellar images, astronomical and mathematical instrumentation, meteoric materials, plants and herbs with stellar attributions.

SYMBOLISM FOR THE DIRECTIONS

Euros – East: Sometimes depicted as a bearded man carrying a cloak, he is often associated with Autumn, so all autumnal symbols, leaves, fruits, nuts and berries are suitable; he is also said to have poured cups of nectar when Demeter visited his father's house, so honey and honey based drinks (such as mead) in glasses would also suffice .

Notus – South: Seen as an un-bearded youth he was depicted with a vase and served water from this vase for drinking when Demeter visited Astraios, pottery and other water receptacles would be suitable symbols; by imperial times there is some evidence that due to his association with the summer months he was also sometimes depicted with a sickle and corn.

---

[32] Dionysica, Nonnus, C5th CE.

Therefore summer fruits and grains and other foliage would also be worthwhile.

Zephyrus – West: Associated with the season of spring, Zephyrus was considered a little effeminate and as such was portrayed as an un-bearded almost androgynous youth. He played music for Demeter when she visited Astraios, so any musical instrument would be good, but reed or pan pipes would be particularly suitable. Spring flowers or any unripe fruits, nuts or other vegetation would also not be out of place.

Boreas – North: Sometimes depicted as an unkempt bearded man carrying a conch shell, suitable symbols at this quarter could be driftwood and seashells. He was also associated with the winter months, so evergreens, holly and winter berries would also be appropriate. He is sometimes also called snake footed, so serpentine imagery would also serve you well.

After the circle and the altars have been laid out you should spend some time balancing yourself using the tetrahedron exercise or another similar exercise of your choice. If you are working alone make sure you have your censer and lustration bowl in front of you; or if working as a group a fellow priest or priestess could process with you carrying them around.

When you are ready, starting in the East and walking round you should first fumigate the boundary of the circle with incense; you could choose to use one of the Hekate incenses listed in the chapter entitled *Incense* or one of your own devising. Upon your return to the East lay down the censer and pick up the lustration bowl and asperge (a stiff bristled pastry brush painted and decorated makes a smashing asperge), again make a full circuit.

Move back round to the centre and face the Olympian Altar, kneel and perform the gesture of summoning followed by the gesture of praise.

At Centre:

> *"I call upon Astraios, king and father of all the winds, hearken unto me, she [or he] who may still the sun and draw down the moon from the sky; summon your charges and stand guardian to this rite."*

A third and final circuit is required, not only to evoke the winds but as a symbolic representation of the ritual purity of the space. During this final circuit, stop and stand facing the direction of the Wind to be called and perform the gesture of summoning (see *Ritual Gestures*):

At East:

> *"I call upon Euros, the luckless, vase bearing God of the East Winds, and humbly request you cease your battles and bring forth the cups overflowing with nectar to bless and preserve this space."*

At South:

> "*I call upon Notus, the destroyer, mistily crowned God of the South Winds, and humbly request you cease your battles and bring forth fresh water to consecrate and purify this space.*"

At West:

> "*I call upon Zephyrus, the messenger, cave dwelling God of the West Winds, and humbly request you cease your battles and bring forth sweet music to fill and sanctify this space.*"

At North:

> "*I call upon Boreas, the devouring one, snake footed God of the North Winds, and humbly request you cease your battles and bring forth ambrosia to feed and sustain this space.*"

CASTING THE CIRCLE – EXAMPLE 2

Another variant of the circle that you may like to try involves a fairly common formula of *voces magicae* within the *Greek Magical Papyri*, Demotic Texts and Curse Tablets. It is based on spell IV.3172-3186 from the *Greek Magical Papyri* and is named as a dream producing charm using three reeds. The manner of preparing the circle is identical to the process described above, with the exception of the altar to Astraios.

The *voces magicae* (also known as barbarous names) used within this rite are fairly common within the *Greek Magical Papyri* and are known as the Maskelli-Maskello formula, they have been included within this circle construction due to a possible connection with Hekate. Betz[33] suggests that the barbarous name *Oreobazagra* may be an epithet of Hekate, although the meaning is unknown, which would certainly appear to make sense as the following name *Rexichthon* can according to the same source be translated as '*bursting forth from the earth*', which is very reminiscent of the title *Nexichthon* meaning '*she who breaks open the earth*', an epithet that has also been attributed to Hekate.

Once the circle is laid out, there are two possible options for which direction to start in. The dream producing spell starts east and progresses clockwise round to south, west and north in the manner of a traditional Solomonic style circle. The other is to correlate four of the *voces magicae* with specific quarters, Betz also suggests that the word *Pypeganyx* possibly means '*Lord of the fount of fire*' which of course would and should be assigned to the Southern quarter. The word *Rexichthon* would obviously correlate with the Northern Quarter and the element of earth, therefore *Oreobazagra* should be assigned the West and *Hippochton* with the East, and according to the order in which the names are recited would imply that you would start at West and circumambulate round clockwise from that position.

---

[33] The Greek Magical Papyri in Translation, Betz, 1992.

Regardless of which direction you start in, fumigation with incense and consecration with an asperge will need to be performed, followed by following formula being called at the respective quarter accordingly:-

At East, whilst performing the gesture of summoning:

> *"I adjure you Lords of the East stand guardian and witness to this rite, Maskelli Maskello Phnoukentabo Oreobazagra Rexichthon Hippochthon Pypeganyx"*

At South, whilst performing the gesture of summoning:

> *"I adjure you Lords of the South stand guardian and witness to this rite, Maskelli Maskello Phnoukentabo Oreobazagra Rexichthon Hippochthon Pypeganyx"*

At West, whilst performing the gesture of summoning:

> *"I adjure you Lords of the West stand guardian and witness to this rite, Maskelli Maskello Phnoukentabo Oreobazagra Rexichthon Hippochthon Pypeganyx"*

At North, whilst performing the gesture of summoning:

> *"I adjure you Lords of the North stand guardian and witness to this rite, Maskelli Maskello Phnoukentabo Oreobazagra Rexichthon Hippochthon Pypeganyx"*

DECONSTRUCTING THE CIRCLE AND THE DISPOSAL OF OFFERINGS

> *"Go away, master of the world, forefather, go to your own places in order that the universe be maintained"*[34]

Once a rite is over, unless you are working in a permanent temple area, it is necessary to return the sacred space you have created back into the mundane world; it would be irresponsible to leave things open and floating around. It's also only polite to thank any entities you have evoked and bid them depart, this includes the quarter guardians and any beings that may have been attracted to the outside of the circle area as a result of the work that might have been undertaken.

There is precedent in three papyri fragments for walking backwards and retracing your steps at the end of a magickal working, one of which is a spell that evokes a Hekate conflation and in one specific line calls Hekate and Hermes together, and a number of the poetic texts and plays bid the person to retrace their steps once the rite to Hekate was over; it was also quite common to bid the God you had called to return to their rightful place, as we can see from the quote above.

Therefore to unwind the circle space it would be prudent to traverse the circle in a reverse direction, starting from east (assuming you started in that

---

[34] PGM IV 3086-3124.

direction), moving through to North, West, South and back around to the East again. As you approach each quarter stand and recite:

> *"I give thanks to you Lord <insert direction or wind name>, return unto your own place and course so that order in the universe is maintained."*

Finally once all the entities have been bid farewell, it is always prudent to perform some magickal as well as physical housekeeping, performing the Eyes of Heaven banishing ritual is an effective way of doing this for it clears the immediate vicinity of any unwanted visitors which may have been attracted by the energies raised during the rite.

It has the added bonus of giving a well meaning but effective shove to any entities summoned who are reticent to depart and didn't take the hint when we bid them farewell. This may sound silly, but it does happen, over the years I have heard tell of a number of rituals where the deity or entity was more than a little reticent to depart; I experienced it myself during an ancestral ritual involving Hekate which involved singing, poetry and plenty of libations; often there is no nefarious reason for this lack of departure after all imagine if you were invited to a party and were having a jolly good time and then the host suddenly decides that it is all over and starts ejecting guests as quickly as possible, if you were having a good time you would be inclined to drag your heels and extend the gathering a little longer, wouldn't you?

PRACTICAL EXERCISE

Try both circle techniques and decide which one fits best with you. Once you have decided which one fits your style, then the only way to memorise it and become proficient is to practise, practise, practise.

KNOT MAGICK AND PHYLACTERIES

"Odysseus hastened to tie the cunning knot which Lady Kirke had brought to his knowledge in other days."[35]

As we can see from the quote above, the use of knots in magick is an ancient thing, and found the world over. Mohammed was said to be cursed by a Jewish wizard who took the prophet's hair and tied eleven knots into it after which his daughter breathed curses upon each knot. Certain Jewish words in the *Old Testament* which have now been translated to mean charmer, specifically relate to knot tying and there are ancient Egyptian papyri that describe how to counteract venom with knots and others that describe the creation of protective amulets which are created by knotting black thread.[36]

The *Greek Magical Papyri* is absolutely riddled with spells and charms that use cords and knots within a wide variety of rites, everything from curing swollen testicles to controlling your own shadow and using it to do your bidding. However, there does seem to be some general correlation as to when cords and knots were used; natural fibres appeared to be the most commonly used, however, red, white and black cords also appear fairly prominently, and these are colours often assigned to Hekate especially in later times.

The following table gives you a list of uses for various threads which you may use in your spells and charms, as you can see some colours overlap with a similar purpose, therefore for general evocation where you wish a deity to aid in the task the knot charm is intended for, then a blue or green thread is recommended. If it relates to general divination or intuition then use red and if it is to become more in tune with the wishes and messages of the Gods then a white thread would be suitable, white threads can also be used much as white candles are often used, as a general purpose colour if you do not have access to the required materials.

How these cords and knots are actually used tends to fall into just two categories: they were either used to tie up or bind a sympathetic object, papyri or metal lamellae inscribed with a charm or they were worn around the body as a type of phylactery, which are best described as protective amulets.

---

[35] Odyssey 8:447 ff, Homer, C9th BCE.
[36] Magic in Ancient Egypt, Pinch, 1994.

Colour	Use
Natural (Undyed)	All Forms of healing, Love, Cursing
Red	Summoning & Divination
White	Summoning & Oracular, General Purpose
Black	Binding & Protection
Green	Summoning
Blue	Summoning
Purple	Oracular

Protection against malicious spirits, unwanted interest, the magickal influence of others and even the Gods themselves was of upmost importance to the magickal practitioner in days gone by and it isn't a subject to be ignored even in this modern day, whilst as a general rule if you find yourself with the sniffles it is most likely you have a caught a cold rather than a curse, just as you create a sacred space to perform ritual, there is no harm in creating a sacred space around your person. This can be done very effectively using knot magick that can then be worn either ritually or even mundanely in a very non obtrusive manner.

The idea behind knot magick is that with every knot or braid created the intent of the magician or witch is bound into the item, often alongside the will of any deity that has been called upon to aid in the task. Chanting can greatly improve focus whilst completing what could be a potentially monotonous and repetitive task and this is probably why weavers and spinners chose to sing as they worked. This technique most definitely appears within the papyri texts, one of which is a general purpose restraining rite which requires the magician to tie three hundred and sixty five knots in a piece of black thread whilst chanting the same *voces magicae* containing Ephesian letters that are also found in the rite of Hekate-Erischigal, which is in itself a protective and initiatory rite.

PRACTICAL EXERCISE - USING KNOTS TO CREATE A PHYLACTERY

Creating, dedicating and consecrating a phylactery is probably the very first magickal act you should undertake before you progress any further, the colours and stones chosen have a specific connection to Hekate so wearing this item during ritual will not only aid in personal protection but also strengthen your bond with the Goddess herself in an act of sympathetic magick.

The materials required to make this object are three lengths of cotton, silk or wool thread (other natural fibres can be used but try to avoid synthetic materials), they should be black, white and red which are colours commonly considered sacred to Hekate. In addition, if you wish to include them, you should have nine haematite or magnetite beads to thread onto and knot into the phylactery; both of these stones have connections with Hekate in the *Greek Magical Papyri* and were used in amulets and talismans.

> *CHANT: ASKEI KATASKEI ERON OREON IOR MEGA SAMNYER BAUI (X3) PHOBANTIA SEMNE (repeat ad nauseum).*

1) Take the three lengths of thread and tie a knot to hold them together.
2) Thread a safety pin through the knot and attach it to a cushion or pillow, this has no magickal purpose other than ensuring stability and giving an even braid.
3) As you start braiding quietly start chanting the *voces magicae* given above all the time focusing on the protective nature of the finished item, from this point on continue chanting until the entire manufacturing process is finished.
4) If you have chosen to bead the phylactery with haematite beads then once you run out of fibre it is time to take the nine beads and thread them onto the braid and tie off the end of the braid.
5) At even intervals secure the beads using a knot, once you have tied all nine beads then the manufacturing process is finished and you may stop chanting.
6) For the period between new moon and full moon wear the item about your person at all times, you are affectively scenting the object with your own energies at this stage.
7) During the full moon consecrate the phylactery for its intended purpose using the rite given earlier, the phylactery is now ready to use and should be worn during ritual and at other times when appropriate.

It is normally considered appropriate to keep consecrated magickal items away from contact with other people, and as a general rule I believe this to be a valid course of action, after all you cannot always vouch for another person's physical, mental or spiritual cleanliness and how their contact will affect the working of the item you have created. However just from a practical perspective there are exceptions to this rule, knot charms, talismans, empowered rings, necklaces and bracelets that are worn on a daily basis for a specified purpose or period of time are likely to from time to time to come into contact with others; as are tarot cards you may use to provide others with readings and ritual tools used in group ritual.

In these cases I would recommend a regime of regular cleansing and re-dedication which can be incorporated into a regular timetable such as quarterly at the Solstices and Equinoxes.

LAMELLAE

An extension of the phylactery is the lamellae, these were usually thin strips of metal, the most common being tin, lead, silver or gold. Usually a charm or spell was engraved with a stylus upon these strips and they were bound to an area of the body or worn about the neck in the style of a necklace; although in some cases such as the ritual of the cat which evokes an aspect of Hekate the lamellae is inserted into or bound around a sympathetic object.

As with the phylactery the lamellae were used for a wide variety of reasons, Tin was the most versatile of metals, although this may have something to do with the cost of the metal rather than some deeply seated magickal power, lead was used almost solely for binding and cursing as was iron. An interesting point of note with iron was that it was also used for spell breaking, so much like various herbal substances which could either kill or cure, metals used in a lamellae could have similar opposing purposes.

Metal	Purpose
Tin	Love & Healing
Gold	Success & Financial
Silver	Memory & Oracular
Lead	Binding & Cursing
Iron	Protection, Binding, Cursing

The lamellae were engraved, often with a bronze stylus, and the engraving could be anything from obscure pictographs, sacred vowels, *voces magicae*, God names and just plain and simple written charms, some of which, particularly in the case of the lead curse tablets, were quite explicit; there is of course a reason for that, we've all been told to be careful what we wish for.

PRACTICAL EXERCISE - CREATING A LAMELLAE

As we have seen above lamellae can be used for any number of purposes from love spells to cursing, and using the table above it would not be difficult to create an appropriate item for your needs. Below are instructions for how to create a lamellae which you may want to wear or bind around a sympathetic object for success.

Obviously hand beating out wafer thin strips of lead, tin, gold or silver is a little bit above and beyond the call of duty, especially with the wealth of hobby shops we now have access to either online or in our local towns, many of which sell *'leaf'* versions of these metals for decorative purposes which can then be glued to thin card and cut to size appropriately, or if push comes to shove card could be sprayed the appropriate metallic shade, remember this isn't all about faithful reconstruction; but that being said if you fancy smelting and creating your own precious metal sheets by all means go ahead but make sure you have the wherewithal to complete the task safely.

> *CHARM:* *Hekate, all powerful in heaven, earth and sea grant me favour in this my request <<insert purpose here and be very specific[37]>>. This, I, <<insert name>> ask you and in return I shall <<insert appropriate offering[38]>> should success be mine.*

1) Choose a metal suitable for your purpose, in this case success in a specific task or endeavour.

2) Using a stylus such as a crochet hook, knitting needle or other pointed object inscribe the charm given above (at other times you may want to adapt the given charm, write your own or use a reduction sigil, instructions for this can be found in the Appendices).

3) Consecrate the lamellae according to the rite given earlier, you may then wear, bury or bind the lamellae as appropriate, in the case of this example if success is required for a job application you may want to wear the item on a knotted cord secreted about your person during the interview, or for a driving test attach it to your car keys.

4) Once the lamellae has served its purpose, destroy or dispose of it appropriately and with consideration for wildlife, burning and scattering the ashes is most probably the best way of doing this, but beware certain spray paints can have toxic fumes when burnt so make sure you do it in a well ventilated area.

---

[37] For example if this was for help passing a driving test you would write something like: that I successfully pass my driving test on xxx date at xxx time.

[38] In ancient times a suitable sacrifice was offered as a bargaining tool, so for example you may offer to burn a candle on her altar every day for a month, or provide her with mead every evening for a week etc.

THE MAGICK WAND

"She touched their faces with her poisoned wand and at each touch each took the magic form"[39]

Whilst many modern pagan traditions rely heavily on the sword or knife as a ritual implement for casting circles, evoking and invoking and for consecrating such things as water and salt, it appears to have only a utilitarian function within Greek magick; and was used primarily for sacrificing offerings to the deity being called upon or appeased.

Wands and branches however, seem to have played a much more central role especially for when calling upon the Gods and daemons to appear in a physical manner. Their function seems to have fallen into two very specific forms, rods or wands of power which were carried by the Gods as symbols of divinity and used by magicians for calling forth the aforementioned Gods or apotropaic items meant to protect the practitioner.

Wands used in this fashion have a long history, Pinch[40] points out that apotropaic wands have been found in ancient Egypt dating back as early as 2800 BCE and suggests that they were used for protection against demons and demarking sacred or protective spaces, a conclusion she draws as the result of a number of these artefacts being scored or marked on one end as if they had been scraped along the ground.

The materials for these wands and protective branches were not very specific, ranging from ebony to olive (wands of the Gods were often described as golden). However, the most common were olive and laurel, although in the case of laurel branches this may have more to do with the function of the laurel leaves themselves rather than the branch they resided upon, for the laurel was sacred to Apollo and often used in divinatory rites.

Kirke, priestess and sometimes daughter of Hekate, possessed a very famous wand with which she was able to perform great feats of magick, transforming Odysseus' crew and other unsuspecting souls into a herd of swine. The wand was also named as a sacred symbol, possibly even an initiatory password within a number of the *Greek Magical Papyri* spells, of which at least three are direct evocations of Hekate or a conflation of Hekate and another Goddess. It therefore seems highly appropriate that a priest or priestess of Hekate should use a wand as a ritual implement over and above any other object.

---

[39] Metamorphoses XIV:387–419, Ovid, 8 CE.
[40] Magic in Ancient Egypt, Pinch, 1994.

PRACTICAL EXERCISE - CREATING A MAGICK WAND

There are a number of myths and legends regarding the manufacture of a magick wand, some traditions suggest ash or hazel as desirable woods, often declaring that the branch from which the wand is fashioned should be cut with a single blow from the tree; and that it should never touch the ground. Mid-summer is often a time cited for the harvesting process, and other traditions place a stipulation that the wood not be harvested by the intended wand bearer.

In reality, as this wand should only be used for rites involving Hekate many of these traditional taboos can be ignored as we have little evidence as to the type of wand Kirke used. Blackthorn or yew might be considered suitable materials for, as we can see from the quote above, Kirke's wand was purported to have been poisonous; however caution should be exercised if you choose either of these particular woods due to potential toxicity. It is preferable for the health of the tree to prune when the sap is no longer rising so, contrary to popular belief, the dark months of the year would actually be a preferable time to harvest whatever wood you wish to use and I would encourage you to consider this fact when you harvest the wood for your wand.

It is advisable to allow the wood you have cut to season and dry out and how you do this can ensure that you have a nice straight wand; tie one end of some string around the end of the wood and the other to a metal coat hanger, so that the wood is hanging down suspended by the string, if you have an airing cupboard (or other warm dry area) then using the coat hanger allow the wood to hang for several months, longer if necessary which is dependent upon the type and thickness of the wood chosen.

Once the wood is dry you may carve, paint or mark the wand with symbols you feel are appropriate to Hekate and your work with her, you can use the table of symbols and items sacred to Hekate provided in Appendix III to help you if you wish; and then consecrate as described in the section on *Consecration*.

PSYCHIC DEVELOPMENT

Everyone has some level of innate psychic ability and the magickal arts cannot be seriously attempted without developing these abilities to some extent. You have already used one of the most basic abilities in the exercises you have already covered, such as the Tetrahedron and casting a circle - visualisation.

The ability to visualise cannot be underestimated, for very few of us will achieve such a level of psychic awareness that we can physically see and touch the Gods, daemons and other spirits that we may encounter in our magickal world. Whilst we may be able to sense a presence with that intangible sixth sense; we will have to rely on our ability to mentally create the images of Astraios and the Winds standing as guardians at our circle edge for example. This ability will make the whole experience more real, and as we shall see later in the book; from time to time an inability to visualise our intended object, or entity may well be our intuition letting us know that something is not right or that we have encountered a new deity or spirit.

You can of course spend hours attempting to visualise different things, such as colours, shapes, animals, food stuff etc. And it is worthwhile at least to have a go at this, but possibly one of the most effective visualisations you can perfect is of yourself. Once mastered, this technique will allow you to move freely into the astral realms, either through a skrying mirror or other astral doorways such as tarot cards.

ESTABLISHING YOUR MAGICKAL SELF

Spend some time looking at a photograph of yourself or better still studying yourself in a full length mirror if you have one, you can do this task naked or dressed in your ritual attire, whichever is most appropriate to the way you work. Really look at yourself, and spend some time describing what you see.

Try to avoid seeing what you think you see, it's very easy for us to have a false impression of what we look like. A good technique to achieve this is to describe to yourself all the things you dislike about your face and body, then repeat the process and describe everything you like about your face and body. This will give you a much more objective image.

Excerpt from Personal Skrying Journal
Needed to spend a while re-establishing my magickal self, I've had issues recently, ever since I had the large mole removed from my side, everything has felt off and askew I've found it hard to visualise from the waist down. Even though I visualise myself with robes, I know that I am also still visualising myself underneath with the mole still there and it almost

becomes a distraction almost like an ache in my side, perhaps this is a bit like the phantom pains that amputees talk about.

Once you feel you have a strong image of yourself spend a few minutes every day for at least the period of one week, preferably longer, it can take months to really establish yourself clearly, sat quietly with your eyes shut, imagine the photograph or the mirror in front of you and reconstruct an imaginary you. Take note of areas you have difficulty with, hair, colour of eyes, hands etc. and continue to examine these paying closer attention.

When you feel that you have at least a passing simulacrum of yourself, start playing with it, make it wave, or nod, say something, you may not hear anything straight away, or you may hear your internal voice which in reality often does not sound like your own, but don't worry. Get it to walk forward and backward, become comfortable with moving this *you* around. You could even try doing a dance or seeing yourself through the eyes of the other you, whatever floats your boat, the point is to construct a sympathetic you with which you can subtly interact with the inhabitants of the astral realms.

Of course it isn't always necessary to use this personal avatar, but it is a very valuable technique that will not only serve us well in such activities as skrying and working within an Astral Temple but will greatly improve our general visualisation skills no end. Therefore it should be practised regularly before going any further and should be revisited on a regular basis, as the above excerpt shows, none of us stay the same physically forever.

INTUITION

Intuition is another psychic ability that should be embraced and practised, as a child I remember my mother's intuition being un-paralleled, but at that time she had little confidence in it and rarely acted upon it. Age and possibly experience has changed that, and my mother's *'spidey sense'* is something that I now rarely ignore.

Children often seem to just know when something is right or wrong, the toddler who for no apparent reason refuses to go near a certain person, or walk down a particular road are excellent examples of their intuition at play. I am of the opinion that we are born with a strong intuitive sense but society does not encourage us to use it and as a result it atrophies, for it is something illogical that cannot be explained with science, or tested empirically with results reliable enough to satisfy the establishment.

Over the years I've heard some wonderful stories as to how this development is achieved, students being given house bricks hidden inside a box and told to meditate upon the contents and report back, matchboxes filled with trinkets and placed inside a pillow case, again with the instruction that using their intuition the student must attempt to divine the contents.

My own mentor provided me with a battered and peeling faux leather briefcase, informing me there was an entity trapped within which I had to deal with, almost immediately I was certain there was no such thing, although the case certainly felt a little funky and off, it was far from inhabited by a denizen of the nether realms; prior to that incident I had unquestioningly followed every instruction given to me and every task followed to the letter of the law, a baby bird swallowing every morsel I was given and it was only when I let my intuition guide me that I started making progress and became an independent magickal practitioner in my own right.

And it is for this reason that developing this skill has remained a fundamental exercise for many pursuing a magickal path; after all when reading the classical texts it never says that Medea or Kirke consulted some ancient magickal grimoire or personal book of shadows, they just knew what needed to be done, intuitively, for Hekate had taught them this skill.

EXERCISE - FINDING LOST OBJECTS

- Choose an object that you have a personal bond with, a favourite book or piece of jewellery would be perfect.
- Ask a family member or friend to hide the object somewhere in your house or garden without your knowledge.
- Quiet your mind and call upon Hekate and Hermes and ask them to aid you in finding the object.
- Either Focus on the actual object itself, imagine how it feels, smells, its natural temperature etc. and see if you can home in on its energy signature.
- Or Visualise handing the person the object and asking them to hide it then let your intuition guide you as to what your friend does with the object.
- Another option is to visualise an area in your house and project your magickal self into a skrying mirror and physically search the astral version of your house for the object, we will cover skrying later in the book so you may want to save this exercise for later.

If you are in the position where it would be difficult to ask a friend or family member to help you with this task, then I would heartily recommend the matchbox exercise, place small trinkets into identical matchboxes, or even slips of paper with different images drawn on them. Place them into a box, pillow case, shopping bag etc. and shake them up, then draw out a single matchbox; again as with the previous exercise quietly call upon Hekate and Hermes for their aid in the task and then meditate upon the contents, write you impressions down in your journal before opening the box to reveal what is inside.

Please be aware however that this is a very specialised skill and some people are far more sensitive to this exercise than others so right from the get go, do not be disappointed if you don't receive mind blowing results, if you manage to even ascertain the rough location of the object or images that relate to the location or contents during your early attempts, then consider that you have done exceptionally well. But you should find that over time and with practise that you improve more than you think even if this skill does not come naturally.

THE ELEMENTS

"The number and the nature of those things, called elements, what Fire, Earth, Air forth brings"[41]

For millennia philosophers and magicians have agreed that the universe consists of four elements, Earth, Air, Fire and Water, they are both physical and metaphysical. And as a result of their dual nature they are one of the most fundamental and readily accessible ways of accessing the magick of the universe, the elements are probably one of the very first things a neophyte must study, I refuse to say master, for you could spend a life time studying the magick of the elements and still be bragging if you said you had achieved more than a general level of competency. I was once told that all I was good for was elemental work, I was devastated at the time, now, well, I take it as a compliment; for the elements are the building blocks of everything that was, is and shall be.

The concept of elements happened way after our first literary reference to Hekate appeared. Empedocles, a pre Socratic Pythagorean is credited with the discovery of elemental attributions of matter. And whilst Hesiod or many of the earlier writers such as Euripides and Sophocles would not have recognised Hekate as having such elemental aspects; this understanding of the world around us, both mundane and otherwise, is, thanks to the great philosophers, so ingrained into the modern world view that it would be remiss of us if we were to ignore it in our quest for gnosis regarding this many faceted Goddess.

Whilst each element is addressed individually in the forthcoming chapter, we should perhaps bear in mind the sage words of Heinrich Cornelius Agrippa, *"For there is none of the sensible Elements that is pure, but they are more or less mixed, and apt to be changed one into the other."*[42] Or put more simply, it is possible, more or less, to isolate each individual element of this Goddess, to work with it individually, to explore her nature and the mysteries she can impart; In fact it is very prudent to do so. But it is necessary to remember that, no element alone is a representation of Hekate in her entirety and most of the historical evidence we can examine regarding her will most likely show more than one of her multiple faces and the lessons she may teach will be as a result of any combination of those faces.

After completing each meditation, do the following exercises, do not worry if the words you receive appear to be nonsense or are even symbols in another language.

---

[41] 3 Books of Occult Philosophy, Agrippa, 1533.
[42] 3 Books of Occult Philosophy, Agrippa, 1533.

1) Write up the experience in your journal, including date, time, planetary hour, day, lunar phase etc. noting anything of significance such as smells, sounds and physical sensations
2) Make a note of the symbols or word you saw upon the door of the chamber
3) Write the word or symbols onto a small clean piece of paper, for the period of roughly one week between full moon and last quarter, carry it with you, think on it, sleep with it under your pillow
4) Make a note of any unusual dreams, synchronicities, unexpected happenings during this time.

HEKATE OF EARTH

> *"That of a dog as having a punishing and avenging nature is raised towards the sphere of earth"*[43]

Earth as an element is considered cold and dry; it is heavy, silent, passive even depending upon which school of philosophical thought you subscribe to. Its planetary aspect is primarily Saturnine in nature. Saturn was the Roman equivalent of the Greek Titan, Kronos, and a thoroughly disagreeable character by all accounts; who plotted with his mother to overthrow his father by chopping off his genitals. He was eventually overthrown by his own son Zeus as the result of committing atrocities worse than his father before him and was imprisoned along with some of his Titan siblings in Tartarus for eternity.

Tartarus, literally means deep dark place and occupies a space below the earth even lower than Hades, Hesiod actually states that "for nine nights and days a bronze anvil might fall from the earth, and on the tenth reach Tartarus". Much like the planet Saturn itself in ancient times was considered the furthest reach of the known heavens; Tartarus was also considered the furthest reach of the earth. Hekate is, in later texts often considered the Queen or Lady of Tartarus and is, according to Iles Johnson citing Plutarch, sometimes considered the judge of Daemonic souls directing them either to Elysium or Tartarus as their actions required.

HEKATE OF EARTH MEDITATION
Planetary Aspect - Saturn
Perfume – Storax or Myrrh

You are walking quietly in a forest, it is early evening and the birds are singing their evening chorus, you feel content, a deep sense of well being fills you. With each step you can feel the ground give very slightly beneath you as the leaf litter on the ground is disturbed by your passing. You hear a

---

[43] Liber De Mensibus, Lydus, C6th CE.

rustle in the undergrowth in front of you and you catch a flash of fur, but it is gone before you can work out what animal it is. Suddenly aware of the wildlife all around, you decide to stand still and see what else there is around, a thrush darts through the leaves searching for a tasty morsel and a crow calls up above.

Presently you notice what appears to be a stand of oak trees tangled and heavy with ivy, running through it is a faint track probably used by the animal inhabitants of the forest and you decide to follow it, sauntering gently almost sluggishly along, allowing your hands to run along the rough bark of the ancient oaks as you go; suddenly you notice that the trees and undergrowth are beginning to thin, and you enter a clearing; it is wide and flat except for a single yew tree in the centre. And although the light is beginning to fade there is still plenty of light left for you to explore this tree and make it home before it is completely dark. So you start walking towards the tree.

When you reach the yew, you decide to rest with your back against it, feeling its age and its wisdom; you raise your head start looking higher and higher into the branches. You notice a single star shining directly above the tree, strangely bright in the dusky sky. Rested you decide to turn your attention to the tree itself, pacing slowly around its vast and ancient trunk. Less than half way round there is a large opening, an opening large enough to let you inside.

As you step inside the opening, you realise that the intertwining roots have created a stairway, descending carefully you count the steps as you go. 1..2..3..4..5..at the fifth step you can just make out a small chamber below, knowing that at any point you could easily climb back up and out, you resolve to progress further, eager to look closer..6..7..8..9..10. Reaching the bottom you look around, the chamber contains four doors evenly spaced around the chamber, unsure which door to try, you briefly examine each one letting your intuition guide you.

Moving closer to the door you have chosen, you then notice a word faintly shining in liquid amber, you take note of this word as it is important and you reach forward to touch the word, but as you touch the word it fades and the door swings quietly open. Walking through you enter a cavern, it is roughly square in shape, with a dark chasm at its centre, in the dim light you can just make out a figure seated on the far side. She looks up and beckons you towards her. So you approach and kneel down beside her. She gestures for you to look into the darkness below, and as you lean forward you realise she has something to show you, so you stare intently letting the vision unfold.

Slowly the vision begins to fade

And as you come to, you realise that the lady is gone and it is time for you to leave. When you feel ready you make your way back through the door and climb the stairs counting them as you go, back into the night air.

Now write up in your journal and complete the exercises as previously discussed.

HEKATE OF AIR

> *"The head of a bull, which snorts like some bellowing spirit, is raised towards the sphere of air"*[44]

Hekate of Air as an element is hot and wet; she is active and light, and her planetary aspect is predominately lunar. As a deity Lunar is most often associated with Selene, the Goddess of the moon and sister of Helios; who, like her sibling drove a chariot across the sky. The chariot was described as being drawn by horses or more importantly on occasion by bulls or cows. She is often depicted with a lunar disk and it is believed that this representation is the reason for her epithet of *'bull horned'*. In later times, Selene was conflated with both Artemis and Hekate

Some people may at this point be scratching their heads, for using some tables of correspondences the moon is normally associated with the element of water rather than air, the Chaldeans appeared to believe otherwise, as the moon is most often discussed in an *'airy'* manner existing neither on the earth, nor in the aether but somewhere in-between.

HEKATE OF AIR MEDITATION
Planetary Aspects – Luna

Perfume – Galbanum or Jasmine

You find yourself back in the clearing, sitting under the boughs of the tree, the air is chill and a little damp, your breath creating steamy plumes as you exhale; staring out into the distance you notice the moon just above the tree line, pale and insubstantial and almost out of its element against the azure blue sky. Your thoughts turn inwards and as you have nowhere to go and nothing to do you sit idly for a while contemplating which of the doors you will venture into today.

The wind stirs the plants on the clearing and you try to identify the ones you can see within your range of vision. Nettle, mugwort, woody nightshade to name but a few, almost ready to doze off you become aware of the sounds you can hear in the distance, a dog barking, the rustle of the wind in the aspen trees on the border of the clearing to the south.

You become hyper aware of every sight, sound, smell, your extremities are tingling, you realise it is time to get up and explore what lies beneath you.

Get up slowly and walk around to the far side of the trunk, and descend carefully counting the steps as you go. 1..2..3..4..5..this time not halting at the fifth but continuing straight down..6..7..8..9..10. Reaching the bottom you look around, for a second you glance at the door you have already passed through, contemplating a return visit, using the word associated with the door to gain access, but the thought passes as you know today is not the

---

[44] Liber de Mensibus, Lydus, C6th CE.

time, another day perhaps, so instead to concentrate on the other doors letting your intuition guide you.

Moving closer to the door you have chosen, you become aware of the word faintly shining in a pale yellow, you take note of this word as it is important, you sigh suddenly uncertain about crossing the threshold and as you exhale the word fades and the door swings quietly open.

The cavern you enter this time is circular, and is illuminated in such a way that there is a peculiar effect of light and dark, you strain your eyes, looking for the lady who inhabits these domains, and there she is, in the distance, naked save for a long string of pearls that are wrapped around her neck and across her waist, her hair wild, she appears lost in total abandon. She is standing before an altar of quartz with a silver dagger in her hands.

You step forward towards her, this time not waiting to be beckoned, understanding your role in this ritual. She nods and passes you a chalice full of dark liquid, it smells pungent, almost minty; you take a sip and then you place it upon the altar and gaze into its depths, wondering what secret it will show you. Breathing slowly you feel the coldness of the liquid you have consumed spreading through your body, you do not shiver but relax into the sensation letting the vision unfold.

Slowly the vision begins to fade. And as you come to, you realise that the lady is gone and it is time for you to leave. When you feel ready you make your way back through the door and climb the stairs counting them as you go, back into cool air.

> *Now write up in your journal and complete the exercises as previously discussed.*

HEKATE OF FIRE

> *"The fire breathing head of a horse is clearly raised towards the sphere of fire"* [45]

Hekate of Fire as an element is hot and dry; she is active and light. And her planetary aspect is predominately martial. As a deity she is the Chaldean Hekate, Hekate Soteira, and the World Soul, the Goddess who carries the weapons of knowledge and arms you to fight the battle of self. To quote the *Chaldean Oracles*:

> *"Being dressed in the full-armoured force of the resounding light, and equipping the soul and the intellect with the weaponry of three-barbed strength. You must cast into your mind the complete synthema of the Triad and wander amongst the fiery rays not in a scattered manner but with concentration"*[46]

---

[45] Liber de Mensibus, Lydus, C6th CE.
[46] Hekate Soteria, Johnston, 1990.

She equips the theurgist with the tools required to undertake their *'God-work'* in a manner most appropriate to time and circumstance, she always asks more than you can sometimes comprehend achieving, but she never gives you more than you can manage for she is about action and doing, success, not failure.

HEKATE OF FIRE MEDITATION

Planetary Aspect - Mars

Perfume – Olibanum or Tobacco

You are standing on the edge of a forest, this time it is dawn, the sky is gray streaked bright red from the rising sun. You have an overwhelming feeling of excitement, you mouth is dry with an almost metallic taste at the back. Today you are going back to the tree and the chamber below. Setting your sights firmly on your goal, you stand tall and stride forward, feeling the power in your body, the strength in your muscles, the blood rushing through your veins; you have a purpose, no time to wander idly towards your destination.

As you get to the clearing and its ancient and solitary occupant the tree, the sun finally clears the tree line, bathing you in warmth and the clearing in an eerie glow. And just for a second the tree, black outlined, appears to writhe almost snake like, blinking to try and clear your eyes you look again, but it is just a tree, standing regally, it's opening already visible, welcoming you in.

Progressing forward, a little more slowly now, you step inside the opening, and descend carefully counting the steps as you go. 1..2..3..4..5..at the fifth step you make out the small chamber below, knowing that at any point you could easily climb back up and out, you resolve to progress further, already contemplating which of the doors you will chose today..6..7..8..9..10. Reaching the bottom you look around, still undecided which door to try, you briefly examine each one again letting your intuition guide you.

Moving closer to the door you have chosen, you then notice a word faintly shining in ruby red, you take note of this word as it is important and you reach forward to touch the word, but almost as soon as you see it the word fades and the door swings quietly open.

Walking through you wonder if you will enter the same cavern as before but from a different angle, but as you step through you realise this is a different place, a different time, the space is triangular in shape, with a glowing hearth at its centre, you can hear bellows somewhere fuelling the flames, rhythmical pounding, there is smoke and heat and in the dim light you can just make out a figure seated on the far side. She is sharpening what looks like a sword, repeatedly placing it into the fire until it glows red hot, working it with a whetstone and then finally quenching it in a receptacle of water. You watch her for some time, engrossed in her labour.

Eventually she looks up and realising your presence beckons you towards her. So you approach and kneel down beside her. She gestures for you to look into the glowing hearth, and as you lean forward you realise she has something to show you, so you stare intently letting the vision unfold.

Slowly the vision begins to fade. And as you come to, you realise that the lady is gone and it is time for you to leave. When you feel ready you make your way back through the door and climb the stairs counting them as you go, back into the warm morning air.

> *Now write up in your journal and complete the exercises as previously discussed.*

HEKATE OF WATER

> *"the head of a hydra as being of sharp and unstable nature is raised towards the sphere of water"* [47]

Hekate of Water as an element is cold and wet; she is passive and heavy. And her planetary aspect is predominately Plutonian. As a deity, Pluto is the roman equivalent of Hades, lord of the underworld and the water of Hekate is subterranean. She is the rivers Styx and Lethe, circling the underworld and the whirlpool of her sometimes daughter Skylla which too can lead to other places.

This is why one of her epithets is enemy of mankind, those whose feet are buried too firmly in the material world cannot achieve balance and she is balance, neither of this world or the other, alive and dead. For just as the waters of the Styx can make you invulnerable, the Lethe can conceal from you the truth; the price you pay the ferrymen, the daemons of Hekate, can determine which of her waters you drink from, those who are not prepared to pay the price for the knowledge she brings could be dragged down into the watery depths of oblivion, for as we all know nothing comes without a price.

HEKATE OF WATER MEDITATION
Planetary Aspect - Pluto
Perfume - Myrrh

You stand before the opening of the tree, cold, wet and tired, your journey today has been hard, the weather inclement, but something has driven you here, despite every shred of common sense telling you to stay home, but you know the time has come to see what is behind the final door.

You enter through the opening and descend carefully counting the steps as you go. 1..2..3..4..5.. 6..7..8..9..10. Reaching the bottom you head straight for the final door, which is inlaid with mother of pearl, iridescent in the dim light. You wonder why you haven't noticed this before. But you know in your heart that it was because the time wasn't right, you were not ready to see it.

---

[47] Liber de Mensibus, Lydus, C6th CE.

You go to reach to touch the word as you have done before, but halt for a second, for there is something different, you can smell something almost sulphurous on the air and upon the door there is a symbol, circular, a serpent consuming its own tail. An ouroboros. Touching the symbol alone does nothing; so you carefully trace it with your fingers, it fades and the word appears in its stead glowing in a deep sapphire blue; and the door swings open.

Before you lies another set of stairs progressing deeper down into the root network of the tree, stepping forward you descend into silence, the last traces of sound from the world above disappearing. You count the steps as you go 1..2..3..4..5..6..7..8..9..10.

As you reach the bottom you realise you are in a Cavern that is so immense that you cannot gauge its shape or size the walls fading into the blackness. Before you is a tree, *'your'* tree but there is something odd, the tree appears lifeless and there is something hanging from it.

You step forward and realise that it is the lady, suspended upside down, one foot bound to a branch. She is hanging limp, un-moving. Stepping closer still you notice she is loosely holding something in each hand. In the right hand a scorpion, in the left a snake. Drawn with an inexplicable morbid curiosity, you step closer still and stare into her stark lifeless eyes which are completely black and fathomless. For you know that it is within her stare that the vision will come.

The vision eventually starts to fade, the lady is still in front of you, but now standing, her eyes are now clear, the most piercing aquamarine, she is smiling at you, you are so close you can smell her and feel her breath upon your cheek, she leans forward and kisses you. You close your eyes for a few seconds, overwhelmed. When you open your eyes, she is gone and you find yourself outside at the foot of the tree, curled up in a foetal position, you are reborn.

Now write up in your journal and complete the exercises as previously discussed.

ORACLES AND DIVINATION

Oracular work and divination was well documented in ancient times, it again fell into the two distinct categories that we examined earlier in the discussion of Greek Magick, namely religious or divinely inspired and sympathetic. We shall be examining both forms of oracular and divinatory work in the following pages.

The sibyls and oracles at various sacred sites could be considered of the former category and were renowned and revered, kings and noble men would often rely upon these often abstract messages, there are a number of direct references in literature that connect Hekate with oracular work. For example, Virgil has his hero Aeneas visit the famous Cumaean Sybil a priestess of Phoebus and Trivia, which is usually considered to mean Apollo and Diana, both of which have close connections with Hekate. And In many of these stories, the priestess appears to provide their Oracles through the medium of trance.

However many of the operations within the *Greek Magical Papyri* fall into the latter category of sympathetic, as the magician often used ritual techniques. Successful outcomes of such rites and operations often relied on appropriate preparations, invocations, times and places along with use of the correct magickal items and sympathetic materials and these techniques can also be effectively used to interact with the various aspects of Hekate.

DAYS AND HOURS OF DIVINATION

> *"You should be aware that there are hours, days and seasons, which are more suitable"*[48]

The *Greek Magical Papyri* contains one fragment, PGM VII.55-167, as seen in the following table, which provides us with an excellent framework for when to perform divination and oracular work on a day to day basis, if for no other reason than to provide a level of control within the practitioner. After all, we've all met that person who can barely make a cup of tea without grabbing the cup to see what omens have been prophesised in the dregs; some will not even start the day without consulting the runes or the cards. It is a fine line between magick and madness and a total reliance on the other worlds is the route that madness takes.

---

[48] The Veritable Key of Solomon, Skinner & Rankine, 2008.

Day 1	At Dawn		Day 11	Afternoon		Day 21	Afternoon
Day 2	At Noon		Day 12	All Day		Day 22	Afternoon
Day 3	------		Day 13	All Day		Day 23	At Dawn
Day 4	At Dawn		Day 14	At Dawn		Day 24	At Dawn
Day 5	At Dawn		Day 15	All Day		Day 25	-------
Day 6	-------		Day 16	------		Day 26	Afternoon
Day 7	At Noon		Day 17	------		Day 27	All Day
Day 8	All Day		Day 18	At Dawn & Afternoon		Day 28	All Day
Day 9	-------		Day 19	At Dawn		Day 29	All Day
Day 10	-------		Day 20	At Dawn		Day 30	Afternoon

As you can see there were actually very few days which were not considered favourable for divination, although the time of day did vary, in addition to this, authors such as Hesiod also believed that certain days were particularly auspicious for certain actions, and even included a section regarding which days were best to perform certain auguries, in Hesiod's case this was Ornithomancy or augury from birds.

PRACTICAL EXERCISE

Initially using a medium that you are currently most comfortable with, for the period of a minimum of three lunar cycles, only perform divination and oracular work according to the framework given. As usual record your work within your magickal journal. After the allotted time frame you should analyse your results to see if specific lunar phases, or certain days of the week give more tangible results, it is important to note these, because playing to your strengths and practising your weaknesses is an important part of working with Hekate, because if you don't do it, she will do it for you.

NOTE: If you do not have a preference or experience with any particular divinatory system, you may want to read ahead first before choosing which method to use.

PLANETARY DAYS & HOURS - TAILORING WORK TO MORE SPECIFIC TASKS

Whilst the structure above is more than acceptable for day to day general work, in the ancient world the seven classical planets were given certain attributes not least of which was a specific day of the week; and magicians even to this day will often perform their rituals according to the correct planetary day and hour. And for very specific magickal work, and this can include oracular work and divination, it is always advisable where ever possible to try and perform this work according to the correct planetary influence. With the advent of the internet calculating these hours is not a particularly arduous task requiring only simple mathematics and the sunrise and sunset times in your geographical location.

Moon (Monday)	Fertility and Birth, Dream Incubation and Clairvoyance, Transformation	Diana Selene Artemis Poseidon Anubis
Mars (Tuesday)	Physical energy, Prowess, courage, conflict, sex, ego, generosity	
Mercury (Wednesday)	Communication, learning, memory, business, divination, Gnosis, secrecy and deception	Hermes Hermanubis
Jupiter (Thursday)	Luck, Truth, Material expansion, Leadership and Authority, Health, honesty, justice	Zeus
Venus (Friday)	Love, beauty, emotions, art and culture, fertility, emotions, friendship, social interaction, bounty	
Saturn (Saturday)	Silence, Wisdom, Teaching, private contemplation, discipline, responsibility, death	Persephone Dionysus
Sun (Sunday)	Wealth, Prosperity, health, Success, confidence, ego	Apollo Helios Demeter

Once we have considered our purpose and chosen an appropriate day, we may like to consider making it even more potent by performing it according to the corresponding planetary hour, These hours are quite simple to calculate, divide the chosen day into 12 equal parts for the time spanning sun up to sun down and again for the duration of sundown until the following sun set, as follows, given a Sunrise = 05:52 and a Sunset = 20:33 there is a total of 14 hours and 41 minutes or 881 minutes of daylight during that day

Divide 881 by 12 = 73 minutes 25 seconds

Therefore each planetary hour for the daylight half of the day is 1 hour 12 minutes and 25 seconds long, a similar calculation can be performed for the night, and owing to the relatively short period of night time in this example the *'hours'* will then be less than the traditional 60 minutes, so if you choose to perform a working at night you may want to consider time restrictions, tipping over into another planetary hour, might produce some unexpected results, a full explanation of how to calculate these hours can be found in Appendix V.

AND FINALLY ON THE ORBITS OF THE MOON

And for the totally pedantic; just as the PGM VII.155-167 provides us with auspicious days for performing divination, the following, PGM III.275-81 and PGMVII.284–99 describe which days are desirable for certain operations, depending upon which star sign the moon is currently in, obviously some are more appropriate than others for modern day magick. The following is mainly interest only, but by all means consider it when you are planning your work.

Aries	Fire divination and love charms
Taurus	Incantation to a lamp (this has been taken as meaning skrying and oracular work)
Gemini	Spells for winning favour and binding spells
Cancer	Creating phylacteries, lamellae and other sacred items; also spells of reconciliation and air divination.
Leo	Creating magickal rings or performing binding spells
Virgo	Anything rendered is obtainable (again this is obscure, but most likely describes the creation of poppets for the purpose of obtaining the real item)
Libra	Necromancy and speaking to other spirits, spells of release (this meaning is unclear but could mean charm breaking)
Scorpio	Invocations and Incantations to the Sun and Moon and charms relating to business transactions.
Capricorn	Anything inflicting evil (baneful magick)
Sagittarius	Say whatever you wish for best results
Aquarius	Love charms
Pisces	Foreknowledge and love charms

The following pages contain information and exercises which aim to allow you perform both religious and sympathetic divination from different elemental perspectives, using tools or techniques appropriate to that element; which in turn can then be used when approaching particular aspects of Hekate. Whilst first becoming familiar with these techniques do not worry about much more than keeping to the correct timetable as given at the beginning, but as time progresses you may like to then utilise the fire methods on fiery days, such as a Sundays and Tuesdays, water methods on watery days and so on. This way, when you start using these techniques in ritual devoted to Hekate it will have become like second nature to you.

Element	Method
Earth	Dice
Air	Skrying (smoke), Tarot
Fire	Skrying (flame)
Water	Skrying (liquid or glass)

DIVINATION - SKRYING

"For now we see through a glass, darkly; but then face to face "[49]

People have been staring into lakes, gazing at clouds and looking for shapes in the fire and smoke and pondering the things they see there for time immemorial. There are very few of us that won't have a childhood memory of looking for dragons in the dying embers of a warm fire on a winter's night, or lying on a piece of grass on a summer's day making shapes from the clouds, letting our minds wander, letting our imaginations take us to places only dreamt of. As children we were, in its most basic form intuitively skrying, tapping into something other than the reality our eyes can perceive.

Skrying can be done in just about any medium imaginable, a mirror, dark glass, water, ink, wine, molasses or black treacle, clouds, flame and smoke. It can be used to divine lost and unknown things; it can be used as a window into the astral realms, to evoke angels and demons or as a method of communication with the divine itself.

There will of course be those who are more naturally adept at these arts, but it is a skill that anyone can learn and gain results with, in some fashion or another. Some will genuinely *'see'* with their physical eyes whilst others will only sense the image in their minds, auditory sensations again may be physical or subtle and with practice the adept skryer will have a strong sense of magickal self and will be able to effectively place themselves metaphysically within the medium; others will, as the quote above quite beautifully puts it be able only to *'see through the glass, darkly'*. This does not mean that the visions will be any less profound or the lessons learnt any less valuable.

Excerpt from Personal Skrying Journal

> *She sits upon a chaise longue, with her upper body turned away from me. Her hair is piled up upon her head in a Grecian fashion. Her left ear has jewellery in it, 5 large garnets set in drops of increasing size. On her feet are sandals of raw leather, cross strapped to just below the knee; she seems not to have noticed me.*

The above is an excerpt from a skrying session that took over an hour, it required a scribe to record the event as it happened due to the sheer length and level of detail; it was planned that way as part of a specific magickal operation. Even three years later that particular session is still being studied and reflected upon.

One of the secrets of effective skrying that is so often left out, is that the analysis of the information you are presented with should happen after the

---

[49] I Corinthians 13:12, C1st CE.

fact, don't try and work it out during the session, it will end in a very short and unsatisfactory experience, you don't sit there giving a minute by minute analysis of your favourite TV programme now do you? You sit and immerse yourself in it; you become one with the characters and identify with the plot.

And when it is over, then you pick it apart! You discuss it with your work colleagues the next day, you snigger over the ridiculous plot twist or the appalling choice the wardrobe department made for the lead actress' outfit.

Now of course skrying isn't quite like that, for a start I really wouldn't be regaling your friends at work with the previous night's adventures, but the process is similar, don't try too hard, don't over think it, or worry about what it means ... if anything; take time to reflect on the experience, document it in minute detail; if you are working alone, then this should be done as soon as possible after the session is over.

You may like to try experimenting with different recording devices, either audio or visual depending upon the type of skrying and the location, although these get mixed reviews, reports of strange background noises, white noise and complete failure are not unknown, so if you break your swanky new gadget you've only yourself to blame as you have been warned and at the end of the day there isn't much that can go wrong with a good old fashioned pen and notebook. But what do you actually *'do'* when you are skrying; everybody talks about it but very rarely is the technique explained in adequate detail. Part of the problem is that the equipment required and the techniques employed really are rather deceptively simple.

HOW TO MAKE A DARK MIRROR

> *"Arise saith the first, move therefore unto his servants; shew yourself in power and make me a strong seething"*[50]

Whilst it is not necessary to make one, many people, myself included prefer to have a dedicated and consecrated skrying tool. Dark mirrors can come in different shapes and sizes and if you look at purchasing one, you may need to reinforce your credit card first because they do not always come particularly cheap. However with a little time and effort a mirror can be made at a fraction of the price.

First you need to decide whether you want a flat mirror, a concave one or a convex one, there is little difference to the technique in using either type; it is mostly about personal preference, both aesthetically and practically. Some people prefer to sky with a flat surface, some with a surface that curves towards you (such people often also like using a crystal ball), and some with a concave surface that has some depth to it and draws you in.

Before you make a decision about which type you prefer, it might be a good idea to experiment with more temporary mediums to give you a feel for

---

[50] John Dee's Five Books of Mystery, Peterson (ed), 2008.

each type. Glasses or bowls of dark liquid such as wine or molasses give a greater level of depth and therefore approximate the sensation of skrying in a convex mirror, whilst any dark flat polished surface will give you the approximation of a flat mirror, I rather enjoyed staring into a brand new and highly polished granite worktop whilst wandering around a *'do it yourself'* kitchen showroom one day which inspired me to try working with an obsidian sphere for a while, a medium I had not previously considered.

Dark Mirror

Once you have chosen which style you prefer the next step is to purchase the appropriate glass, flat is obviously the easiest to source for any glass or Perspex fronted picture frame will suffice, these can be found readily in hobby shops, charity shops and flea markets for next to nothing. Convex is a little harder to source, my mirror was created from an antique 13" Grandfather clock face which was purchased second hand, but they really don't have to be as large as this. Any old clock with a glass face could be dismantled to procure the glass, many electric clocks from the 1950's had convex faces and these can be found regularly in charity shops and online auction houses, the one criteria when purchasing one of these clock faces is, that, it should be as scratch free as possible.

The next stage is to clean that sucker within an inch of its life, preferably wearing lint-free gloves if you have them to stop fingerprints, smudges and smears; a solution of spirit vinegar and hot water is an excellent way to do it, then polish it with old newspaper for a pristine shine, it works, better than most proprietary glass cleaners, ask your grandma, I bet she knows all about it. You are ready then to progress to the next stage. This is to either back it with some kind of dark fabric or paint.

The fabric backing really only works with the flat mirrors, a felt or velveteen works well, at a push of course you could just use black sugar paper but that often leaves it looking too flat, the material tends to add an extra dimension to the finished effect. Paint can be a better option as it is effectively then bonded to the glass, and gives a more even finish; this is the technique you need to use with convex mirrors, spraying or painting the underside of the glass (not the top). Blackboard paint is excellent, as is some of the smooth coat enamel sprays, even acrylic artists paints can be used but that can be tricky and will require a number of coats, the first will be very streaky. Of course the same principles can be applied to a convex mirror, but working on the other side of the mirror to how you do for a convex one.

Once the glass is dry then flat mirrors can be simply mounted back into the frame, which you may or may not have chosen to decorate in a style of your choice. Some people will paint or stick planetary symbols, sigils and other magickal insignia onto the back of the mirror prior to mounting but this is entirely up to you, consecration and dedication will be more than sufficient for most purposes.

The convex mirrors are a little trickier to mount, if you are lucky then the clock face will still have the brass bezel intact which will protect the edges, however often this is not the case, so the best bet to protect what is normally very delicate edges, is window leading, hobby shops sell rolls of this stuff which come with an adhesive back so that it will stick directly onto the edge of the glass and then fold round to protect the entire edge and layer up to give extra protection. Storing convex mirrors is also a consideration, old hat boxes are a really good option and you can even buy new ones in some of the larger hobby shop chains. All in all whilst stunning and very enjoyable to use, the convex option is harder to create and store, but they can look absolutely stunning.

Once your mirror is complete you should dedicated it and consecrate it using the ritual given in the section on consecration earlier in this book.

GENERAL SKRYING TECHNIQUES

Preparation

Firstly you need to choose an appropriate medium in which to skry, as discussed in the introduction to this chapter, each of the techniques being covered is ultimately aimed at you, the practitioner, accessing an elemental aspect of Hekate using the correct elemental medium, in this case skrying is considered a water or fire element so the choice of tool should either be of a liquid nature, or of a fiery nature.

Possible choices for a watery medium could be a glass of red wine, a bowl of water with a dark ink colouring it, treacle or a dark mirror, the construction of which has already been covered; glass is after all a liquid, if an unusual one. Fiery mediums could be a candle flame or an open fire if you have access to one either indoors or out. Another option is *'fire-gel'* in a suitable receptacle, although obviously extreme caution should be exercised when dealing with fire indoors, burnt altar cloths are really no fun and potentially very dangerous and are a guaranteed way to cut your skrying short as you hop around the room whacking at whatever is going up in flames.

Whether you choose to place your skrying medium on a constructed altar or just a solid base is entirely up to you, sessions do tend to be more effective in low light, candle light being ideal, although if you are using a watery medium you may find you get better results if the candles are positioned some distance away and at a lower level than the skrying tool itself as it stops light reflections bouncing off the surface which can be very distracting.

Without a doubt the very next stage of the process can be considered a bit like a pre-flight check that ensures that everything is running smoothly, and practically everybody agrees on this stage, which is, perform some kind of banishing ritual, whether that is the banishing ritual provided in this book or some other ritual designed with a similar purpose in mind such as casting a protective circle which we have already covered. What you are doing is making sure that you aren't going to take things through with you that are already hanging around.

STATING YOUR INTENT

Random unfocused skrying can be very entertaining, but often that is all it is. Having a specific purpose in mind and calling upon deity to aid in the task is often not only helpful from a consistency perspective, but can aid in ensuring that there is little interference from unwanted sources. I have found Hekate to be an excellent deity to call upon when embarking upon skrying sessions as she was often called upon in the ancient texts to send visions and to announce to the enquirers what would come to pass[51] and her priestesses were known to foretell the future with her aid; from personal experience I can say this aspect of her has proven to be just as powerful and effective thousands of years later.

Therefore once comfortable and ready to begin you may like to use the formula given below, which is an adaptation of an evocation which is found in the *Greek Magical Papyri*, or if you feel comfortable enough, you may like to write your own.

> *"I call upon you, Mother of all men, you who have brought together the limbs of Meliouchos; I call upon you, Entrapper, Mistress of Corpses, Hermes, Hekate, Hermekate; I call you, come to me to aid me in my magickal work; for I wish to <<<insert statement of intent here>>>, Hermes, Hekate, Hermekate heed me.*[52]

PROCEDURE FOR PRODUCING VISIONS

If your magickal practises up until now have involved spending considerable time studying and performing the asana techniques of pranayama yoga then feel free to skip the next paragraph or two as a small

---

[51] Paean 2, Pindar, C5th BCE.
[52] PGM III.1-164.

amount of physical discomfort is likely to mean nothing to you and you can choose to position yourself anyway you like; but for the rest of us mere mortals the following tips can help ensure the ability to skry for extended periods of time.

However you choose to seat yourself, the ideal is to have a straight back and not be so comfortable that you are likely to fall asleep; so you may need to experiment with a number of different positions before you find the right one for you.

One of the easiest ways to sit reasonably comfortably, if you can manage it, is to sit cross legged, but be aware that the weight of your knees on your ankles and feet may cause pins and needles over time and that can be extremely painful. Meditation stools and cushions are an excellent way of seating yourself cross legged if you have one, because they can stop this from happening; but a good straight backed chair is also a really good way to sit comfortably, just ensure your feet can rest flat on the floor, if your legs are dangling, the pressure of the chair edge on the back of the thighs can also cut off the circulation to your lower extremities.

The mirror or other skrying tool should be no more than 30 to 50cm away from your eyes for best effect; this can be placed on a table in front of you, held in your hands or on a low altar if you are sitting on the floor. This can vary slightly depending upon the medium, if you are using an open fire or fire gel then sitting further back is sensible for a number of reasons, most of them safety related.

The technique for actually looking into the medium also varies a little depending, for liquids the trick is not to actually focus your vision on the surface, but much like those *'seeing eye'* posters that were popular in the 1980's you should stare through the surface imagining a focal point a short distance behind, say maybe 10cm.

For a candle flame it's not really advised to stare for long periods of time directly at the flame itself, although retina burn is highly unlikely you may be seeing spots in front of your eyes for a long time afterwards if you try skrying this way. Instead focus your vision a few millimetres above the flame, in a still and calm environment you will see that there is an aura or void area that surrounds the flame, this is the ideal focal point. When using an open fire, the ideal is to stare into the embers or the source of the flame rather than watching the flames themselves, although, that can also produce results; you will need to experiment with this and take notes.

And finally: DON'T FORGET TO BLINK! You blink all the time when seeing with your mundane eyes, so why should blinking affect your visions on the astral. In truth your actual eyes are a bit surplus to requirements as it isn't really them that are doing the seeing when you skry; unless of course you are extremely sensitive; but either way you need to look after them and blinking is a natural bodily function that enables that.

TESTING THE VISIONS

> *"What is your divine name? Reveal it to me ungrudgingly, so that I may call upon [it]"*[53]

For the most part, especially during the early days of skrying it will seem more like viewing through a dark window or a television screen, especially until you get a strong sense of your magickal self, and start working with specific entities, but before that happens (and even after), if you do come across an entity you need to make sure they are genuine and deal with them appropriately.

Morality on the astral planes has always been a hot debate, there are those that will tell you that the other worlds are filled with wondrous beings full of divine light working tirelessly for the good of mankind, others will say that the spirits of the other worlds are dark and evil, ready to cling to you and cause you harm. As always the truth lies somewhere in between and isn't always as easily explainable.

The first stage is to realise that the morality system we hold so dear means nothing to the denizens of the other worlds. Ask the local nature spirits to help you clean up your local river bank, and they may well respond, but the simplest solution is to get rid of the perpetrators of the pollution problem isn't it, it's not wicked it's not evil, it makes sense even, cure a problem at the root. So don't be surprised if you start hearing of a spate of mishaps around dusk in that spot, no seriously!

The same applies with the entities you will from time to time meet whilst skrying, whether it is through liquid, flame, tarot or other, there does not seem to be a particular medium where a practitioner is more prone to anomalies. Sometimes these entities will not be who or what they appear to be, or act in a manner that appears alien to our sensitive moral structure, and ascertaining what they are and what their intent is, forms a fundamental part of the skrying process itself, as fundamental as taking a ritual bath and in many ways for the same purpose.

Once the skrying session has begun, there are a number of schools of thought regarding this testing procedure, some advocate firing various invoking and banishing pentagrams and hexagrams at the entities you encounter along your journey, but somehow this seems at best discourteous and at worst a violent and extreme reaction, the best analogy would be this. You see your favourite celebrity walking down the street towards you, and out of the blue they stop to talk to you, it may just be asking for directions or asking the time of day, but they've stopped to talk to YOU. What an excellent opportunity to say you've met this person, so you aren't going to go fishing into your handbag or coat pocket for a can of pepper spray and point it at their face demanding that they prove they are said celebrity before you respond, now are you? Well, unless of course you enjoy collecting restraining orders!

---

[53] PGM I.42-195: A spell for acquiring an assistant.

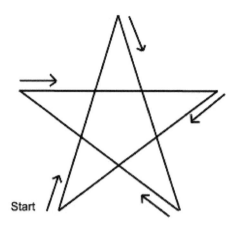

Banishing Earth Pentagram

In the first instance testing entities can be far more courteous than the metaphysical version of the latest computer game involving laser guns and high tech gizmos, leave the heavy duty ceremonial stuff until you haven't got another option. Very few genuine entities will mind being tested in such a manner, even Hekate herself; some may also demand it of you in return so that a rapport can be built, passwords or symbols or signs can be exchanged so that you do not have to go through the rigmarole of testing all over again at a future time. This softly, softly, approach can also then allow for chance encounters being beneficial, said entity may not be what you were hoping for or expecting, but you know, they may still have something interesting to say.

The Process of Testing

Step One: Ask the Entity if they agree to be tested?

If they decline, banish and exit

If they accept move onto step two

Step Two: Ask Entity for their name and any affiliations they may have? (For example Hekate might respond that she is Hekate daughter of Asteria and Perses, honoured most highly by Zeus)

a) If they decline, banish and exit

b) If they accept and give an answer move onto step three, with the caveat that at this stage said entity could be lying, so use your intuition, if it doesn't feel right perform option a) and try again another day.

Step Three: Ask Entity to swear upon their identity that their responses to you will always be truthful?

a) Again, if they decline banish and exit

b) If they accept move onto stage four, but again with the caveat, be very careful to listen to exactly what they say, it has been said that the Goetics are hell's lawyers, and this may well be true for the devil is in the fine detail, do make sure they are actually swearing to the above.

Step Four: Introduce yourself in a formal manner (see examples below), you can do this even if the entity isn't who you were expecting, you never know when they might come in handy. Also give them a password and two questions with which you will know them in future encounters.

a) If it was the entity you were expecting then interact with them at will

b) If not and you do not wish to talk to them; then ask them to depart in peace. This may herald the end on the skrying session, it may not, you will have to suck it and see. But now a protocol has been established should you wish to ever call this entity again you will be able to do so and quickly ascertain that they are what they appear to be through the password and question validation system.

Formal Introduction Example One (to be used if you have no magickal affiliations)

I am *<<Give Full Name>>,* whose father is *<<Give Fathers Full Name>>* and whose mother is *<<Give Mothers Full Name>>,* I give you this so that you may know me and come when I call.

(At this point you may want to give a password and questions if you wish to deal with them again).

Formal Introduction Example Two (to be used if you have a magickal name or affiliations)

I am *<<Give Full Name>>,* whose father is *<<Give Fathers Full Name>>* and whose mother is *<<Give Mothers Full Name>>,* who is known by *<<Give Magickal Name or Motto>>* and whose title is *<<Give grade, degree or other such "rank" as is appropriate to your tradition>>* in the *<<Give the Tradition Name>>* Tradition, I give you this so that you may know me and come when I call.

(At this point you may want to give a password and questions if you wish to deal with them again).

One last word on this subject before moving on; just because an apparent entity declines any of the testing above do not necessarily assume that it is out to get you or cause you trouble, a magickal practitioner's biggest enemy is themselves, and this apparition may be of your own making which is why it is unable to answer. It is the other reason for making testing part of your usual skrying routine, which is, that it helps to keep you real and stops you running wild with imaginative flights of fancy.

Finishing the Session

Once your skrying session is over good housekeeping is again the number one priority, thank any spirits present for their time and ask them to leave in peace, deconstruct your circle, and also perform a banishing if the energy in anyway feels a little *'funky'*. Clear up offerings and dispose of them suitably.

And finally if you are using a crystal, mirror or any other permanent skrying device, cover it up. Consider your skrying mirror to be a bit like an astral budgie cage, if you want the residents to stop tweeting then cover them up.

PRACTICAL EXERCISES

By now you are probably wondering what the heck this all has to do with Hekate, other than the fact we can call her to aid us in our task when performing general skrying operations; well it's quite simple really, skrying is one medium in which you can interact with your chosen deity, either through visions or full on evocation but in a *'sandbox'* like environment, it is after all not always convenient to be summoning up deities in your front room especially when the rest of the family is watching their favourite soap opera. You can of course do all this in an astral temple (which we shall be looking at in a later chapter), but even that can be a bit of overkill and besides which it has other useful purposes as we shall see.

But once you are comfortable with the whole process of skrying the next logical step is to actually interact with the Goddess herself in a more intimate manner and an excellent way of doing this is to petition her to reveal your personal daemon should you wish to do so.

One word of caution is required however, do not expect instant results for this; it may take weeks possibly even months before you receive this gift and you do need to make sure that you are ready for what you are asking for.

Step One - Interacting with Hekate

This exercise can be worked upon at any time (and independently of your petition for those who do not wish to perform the full rite), but you may like to incorporate your first attempts into either the standard Full or New Moon rituals given in the next chapter.

For this exercise, it is wise to use a more specific evocation than the one we have previously used, the one given below is quite suitable, but as time goes on and you wish to interact with specific aspects of Hekate, you may want to write your own and if this is your first ever actual interaction with Hekate, then standard testing procedures should apply.

> *"Maiden Goddess of the watery, earthly and fiery realms,*
> *I call you,*
> *Mother of the Mysteries,*
> *Bring me a vision,*
> *Torch bearing fire bringer,*
> *Show me your form, speak with me,*
> *Be with me now and reveal your secrets"*

What unfolds may be an actual image of the Goddess herself or she may choose to show you images or scenes that will teach you something, when the visions fade make sure you thank Hekate for whatever she has shown you, even if it has left you scratching your head and wondering what the hell it was all about. Normal housekeeping and writing up of experiences then applies; this exercise should be performed initially at least once a month for six months before you progress to the next step.

Step Two – Petitioning Hekate

By now you should be more than comfortable with skrying and also calling upon Hekate to manifest in vision form now is the time to petition her to reveal to you your personal daemon. As we are now working with a very specific intent a more specific evocation is required, I will be honest: I am loathe to give you a specific formula for this part of the operation; personally I was given a dream that repeated itself night after night until I acted upon the instructions in the dream, in it I laid out stuffed toys in a bizarre array of shapes and sizes in a 7x7 grid to which I seemed to bow down and show deference to. What resulted was an operation based upon the Jewish concept of the 50 gates of wisdom and understanding which is supposed to represent the 49 days the Israelites wandered through the wilderness led by Moses to Mount Sinai where on the 50th day they received the Ten Commandments and subsequently built the Ark of the Covenant.

Therefore I am going to leave you a little high and dry and suggest that at this point you consider writing your own petition based upon your own personal motivations for wanting to have access to this entity; this might be the only time I say it, but sorry folks if you're meant to do it, you will find a way.

DIVINATION - TAROT CARDS

Tarot is a form of divination that is centuries old, the earliest decks are beautifully illuminated pieces of art from Renaissance Italy. It was believed that these decks were commissioned by local nobility as playing cards, but over time they have become synonymous with fortune telling and divination and the occult. Much of the reason for this may well be the mapping of the 22 cards from the major arcana or trump cards onto the pathways of the Qabalistic Tree of Life. And it is probably this syncretisation that leads people to believe the cards are much older than they actually are. The lack of millennia old provenance does not make them any less valid though, particularly as their use in the occult arts has been documented for much longer than most modern magickal traditions and orders have been in existence.

But what is the Tarot and what makes it such a useful tool when working with Hekate? And other deities for that matter!

It would be easy to gloss over this section as it is almost inconceivable that somebody interested in magick and the occult hadn't at least a passing familiarity with a deck of tarot cards, but if a job is worth doing, it's worth doing well, and over the years it has become obvious that it is these assumptions and the subsequent corners being cut that can lead to problems later down the line. Many experienced practitioners will, from time to time, take stock of what they have learnt, what they haven't, what they need to, and what they have forgotten altogether and in fact Tarot is an excellent medium with which to do this. So for the experienced practitioners out there do not expect any recommendation that you skip or gloss over this section, you need to do the work too, remember nobody is so experienced that they can't learn something new.

THE MINOR ARCANA

In its most base form the Tarot are a deck of cards which are split into two distinct parts, normally referred to as the Major and the Minor Arcana, the Minor Arcana most resemble our traditional deck of playing cards, there are four suits, normally named, wands, coins (or pentacles), swords and cups, like traditional cards they contain ten pip cards from the ace through to the ten, in additional they usually have four court cards, the knight, the page (or sometimes the princess), the queen and the king. Each suit represents a particular elemental attribution, earth, air, fire and water which we have already come across in an earlier chapter and in each elemental suit each card is given a particular meaning or set of meanings. Conventionally the Minor Arcana are considered to represent the little things in life and the finer detail.

THE MAJOR ARCANA

In addition to the recognisable suits the Tarot contains twenty two extra cards, which are numbered from zero through to twenty one. In traditional tarot reading, the Major Arcana are often associated with the big picture, the large and important things which need to be addressed sooner rather than later. These too have planetary, elemental and astrological attributions which an experienced reader will take into account when performing a reading for a friend or client, however, for our purposes this is not an area we need explore too much further to complete the practical exercises. It would be worthwhile for anybody wishing to develop this work further to learn these correspondences and work with them to enhance their understanding of both the cards and of Hekate herself.

PRACTICAL EXERCISES

The Tarot is an excellent medium for meditation, and aiding in a form of astral travelling. And it is these latter uses that we shall primarily concern ourselves with for the remainder of this section as the Major Arcana particularly is a great tool for understanding various aspects of Hekate.

Please make sure you have a tarot deck to hand, it needs to be a Rider Waite or a clone of a similar ilk so that you can adequately access the symbolism. The Rider Waite has been chosen specifically for this exercise as, not only is it (and its derivatives) one of the most popular decks in the world today but the cards were specifically designed with western esoteric symbolism and practise in mind, whereas the earlier decks such as the Tarot of Marseilles were based more upon the earlier game playing decks from the mid 15th century.

The following descriptions are not only intended as ways of learning Hekate's aspects through meditation, but also can be used as descriptions of astral doorways which one can use to access the other-worlds, and they can even be learnt and used in a divinatory manner as part of (or preparing for) ritual relating to Hekate as we shall see at the end of this section.

USING THE TAROT TO UNDERSTAND ASPECTS OF HEKATE

0 - The Fool

The fool is a representation of beginnings, choices that can be made and directions that can be taken; he has the Zen of the beginner's mind, where anything is possible. Hekate's beginning as we most clearly understand it started out very similarly; she set forth from her cave, her quest to find the Goddess Demeter and bring news of her daughter. Unlike Helios who chose to keep his own council until asked, she decided unbidden to share her knowledge.

The image of the fool is not dissimilar to the early Hekate, we see a golden haired youth holding a white rose, a symbol of virginity and purity, across his shoulder he carries a staff, which could easily double as a torch, his head is actually turned away from the sun, carefree unconcerned as to the sun's reaction once the knowledge has been passed on. At his heels a young white puppy dances playfully, perhaps the only indicator of the metamorphoses that will occur as the result of this journey.

> *I call upon tender hearted Hekate. Daughter of Asteria and Perses, bring me your pearls of wisdom as I embark upon my quest for gnosis*

1 - The Magician

The fool becomes more experienced and as a result gains awareness of his potential and power, he masters the elements and controls the material world around him. Hekate finds this potential in the works of Hesiod, she has retained her Titan powers and controls the elements of earth, air, fire and water, and with this she can aid those who choose to petition her.

We now see a more mature Hekate represented in the image of the magician, still adorned with a bright band around her head, and wielding a wand which is still reminiscent of the torches she carries; the symbols of her privileges in the earth air and sky are laid before her, the pentacle, the chalice and the sword. We see the snake imagery starting to show through with the snake that encircles her waist and the roses around her are now red; a symbol of passion, less innocent, sometimes fickle, but still a strong symbol of intent.

> *I call upon the earthly, watery and celestial dame. Hekate, grant me your favours, so I may come into my power and reach my potential.*

2 - The High Priestess

Worldly wisdom is only part of the picture, the fool encounters the spiritual realms upon his quest, the realms of intuition and magick, logic becomes warped like a landscape upon a moonlit night, when nothing appears exactly as it does in the cold light of day. Hekate slips into her nocturnal role willingly as the oracular Goddess of magick, as the maiden with the ruddy feet who predicts the future and that Pindar wrote so eloquently about.

The Priestess card shows this progression from day to night, the pillars on either side of her, show the light spread by her illuminating torches and also the shadow that is cast, Hekate now wears upon her head a lunar crown and she sits between the otherworld which is depicted by the veil adorned with pomegranates, for beyond lies the realm of Hades and Persephone and she alone is the guardian of the threshold and the voices that whisper from beyond. The equal armed cross upon her breast is a solar symbol hinting upon her earlier lighter aspects, the sun and logic and the moon and intuition and understanding currently perfectly balanced.

> *I call upon Hekate before the Gate; she who stands as guardian to the mysteries, grant me an Oracle of understanding.*

3 – The Empress – A perfect balance and logic and intuition can bring great creativity, growth, luxury and abundance; and the Empress card epitomises these gifts. She is rich and sensuous, wife and mistress, mother and nurse. We first see these traits in the Hesiodic Hekate, who can bestow abundance, victory and rich gifts to those that call upon her, and later these traits are further refined in the Orphic hymn to the Goddess Prothyraea who is considered an aspect of Hekate for she shows similar traits; she is described as a benevolent nourisher who holds nature's key, which of course is reproduction.

The Empress sits regally upon a richly adorned throne, holding a royal sceptre, again the comparison to Hekate's torch should not be ignored, and upon Hekate's head is a crown of stars, the symbol of the authority she also maintains in the heavens and her mother's gift to her; the starry night. Life springs up around her fed by the waters of life, ripe wheat carpets the foreground, a strong symbol of the connection Hekate has with the mysteries of Eleusis and the sacred rites of Demeter and Persephone.

> *I call upon Hekate who is honoured most amongst the Gods. Who from the beginning has been nurse of the young. Bestow upon me your blessings.*

4 – The Emperor – Creativity, fertility and abundance requires a level of structure and control or the garden of paradise that the Empress resides within will grow unruly and wild; chaos will eventually ensue in the glut of decadence. The Emperor commands that order be maintained, if need be through physical action. This is the Hekate we find in Ovid's *Metamorphoses*, she aids Medea in many a nefarious task, yet still she has strictures and guidelines, she has forbidden her priestesses to return a soul to the living if they have passed their allotted time, she understands the order of things.

The throne of the Emperor is not the opulent chaise longue on the Empress, although it is richly carved, it is un-cushioned showing a level of austerity, in his right hand he holds a sceptre reminiscent of the Tau cross, a cross of three ways, the dominion of Hekate. The Chaldean Hekate portrays the martial role an Emperor has to play as depicted by the armours showing through underneath his rich yet subdued garments, for she is described as being a Goddess in full armour and carrying weapons, a hint at the force with which she is prepared to deal with those who do not heed her messages.

> *I call upon Hekate, invincible Queen, who sits by kings, judge me wisely and with compassion and aid me if it is your will.*

5 – The Hierophant – Whilst the Emperor and Empress nurture the physical needs of their people, the Hierophant is the spiritual guide and teacher; people come to him for advice, knowledge and understanding. This is the Hekate of the temple, the establishment, the Goddess who Medea spends her days serving. She is also the mentor that teaches magickal arts and as a result takes her traditional and rightful place in the household shrine.

The hierophant sits between two pillars of stone, these are not ethereal pillars of dark and light such as we saw with the High Priestess, but instead of stone, these are temple pillars, representative of an established religious building, the temple. Raised above the two figures below, we see the Hierophant dispensing a sermon to the figures knelt below him, Hekate teaching her witches Medea and Kirke. Again we see a sceptre, this time with horizontal bars crossing the vertical, a hint towards the Chaldean Hekate, who sits and mediates between the Empyrean, Ethereal and Material world.

> *I call upon Hekate of the Empyrean realm, whirling, holding and perfecting; be a conduit for me and teach me your secrets.*

6 – The Lovers – All about union and partnership both physical and intellectual, the lovers teach the fool the importance of the decision to unite logic and emotion; and how this can affect the path we take. This is the Hekate who aids Medea with her magick, the ultimate conclusion of which is the union of Jason and Medea, who themselves represent the masculine and feminine aspects of the whole.

The lovers stand naked turned towards each other, the female, beside an apple tree with a serpents coiled around it, again a hint to Hekate's serpentine nature; the male stands beside a tree that appears to be adorned with flaming leaves, these trees remind us of Psellus' description of Hekate; who states that her right side is the source of souls, and the left the source of virtue. Of course the tree growing beside the female is also the tree of knowledge of good and evil found in the bible, but does this mean that her serpentine nature is inherently evil, most certainly not; the serpent may provide the knowledge and present us with the ubiquitous crossroad but it is our free will that chooses what to do with it.

> *I call upon Hekate and Hermes united as Hermekate, communicate to me the paths I may travel and guide me to a harmonious and loving existence.*

7 - The Chariot – The chariot and the charioteer are symbols of victory and the reward of the hard work and dedication required to achieve success; however, it takes discipline to control the unruly steeds pulling the chariot, just as it takes control to master dealing effectively with the unforeseen obstacles that life often throws in the way of our best laid plans. This aspect of Hekate is an extension of the Hekate we have already seen portrayed in the Lovers card; she is willing to stand by Medea as she comes into her power and opposes her father to aid Jason in his apparently impossible task.

The Charioteer is adorned with the victor's laurels, but yet he doesn't smile, his face is composed into a visage of intense concentration, he is physically restrained, no whooping of wild abandon for him, quite possibly because he is aware of the chastising aspect of Hekate who is more than happy to express her displeasure at ill-conceived and thought out actions. We see this in Apollonius' *Argonautica*, when Selene (who later becomes conflated with Hekate) expresses her displeasure at being drawn down from the sky so often, to aid Medea in her work, we also see it in Hekate's speech in Shakespeare's *Macbeth*, where she admonishes the witches for performing magick without her aid.

> *I call upon Hekate of the ways; accompany me on the path less travelled and illuminate it for me so I may traverse forward unhindered.*

8 – Strength – This card is all about courage and stamina, it is not about physical strength but inner strength and beauty which can move mountains and tame unpredictable lions. Whereas the Chariot requires the use of the rod, strength can indicate that a velvet glove can often be just as effective. This is Hekate as Potnia Theron, the mistress of the beast, an echo of which we see in her daughter/priestess Kirke who bears the same epithet, she overcomes Odysseus' crew with charms and incantations not brute force.

We see a maiden dressed in a pure white robe, crowned with a garland of flowers, gently opening the mouth of a lion, a symbol of power, strength of passion; the whole scene corresponds with the *Chaldean Oracle* of Hekate who claims that if you call upon her often *'you will perceive everything in lion form'*. The original name for this tarot card was fortitude and in many ways this is a better expression of the meaning of this card when exploring the mysteries of Hekate, as fortitude and gentle persistence are necessary virtues that a magickal practitioner must possess in order to learn her secrets and step closer to the state of henosis.

> *I call upon Hekate, Mistress of the Beasts; show unto me your lion forms so I may overcome my battles and weaknesses with gentle persistence.*

9 - The Hermit – Just as a hermit in real life withdraws from the material world, to contemplate the deeper mysteries, so too does the Hermit in the tarot deck. The quest for knowledge and union with the divine is as much an inward journey as it is a journey through the world and success may require deep soul searching and removing irrelevant things that clutter your life. This is the Hekate that the Cumaean Sybil summons in the darkened grove prior to beckoning Aeneas forth into the underworld.

We see a grey shrouded figure standing upon a mounting top, the figures eyes are closed, head bent in contemplation, there is almost an air of resignation and fatigue about the stance, as he grasps with his left hand a staff for support, and in his right hand he holds a lantern with a star aloft. The lantern and the star it contains is Hekate Phosphoros, she can illuminate and guide him, a beacon of hope in an otherwise darkened world; the Hermit stands patiently waiting for spiritual inspiration to strike and this is often how Hekate operates, for just as when you call upon her things appear in *'lion form'* the same oracle states that *"all things are seen by flashes of lightning"*.

> *I call Hekate, bearer of light; shine your torches like a beacon so that I may use it as a point of focus as I contemplate your mysteries.*

10 – The Wheel of Fortune – Also known as fate, the wheel of fortune turns with the fool travelling upon it, riding the cyclical nature of life, fortunes both good and bad; he travels this wheel out of necessity as does every person who wishes to gain a closer understanding of the divine. The wheel is a symbol of the strophalos of Hekate that Psellus informs us we should labour around and also of the Iynges which were oracular daemons that travelled between humanity and the Gods and vice versa, these entities were, under the jurisdiction of Hekate under the Chaldean system of Magick.

On the card we can see the wheel placed centre stage, written inside it is the word Rota, which means to spin or to turn, this reminds us of the whirring and turning motion of both the strophalos and the Iynges. Operating the strophalos was said to compel the Gods to descend from the heavens even against their will; an operation which could well be fraught with ups and downs for the will of the Gods is not always a thing to trifle with. Surrounding the wheel we see three figures, riding the wheel as it were, sitting high on the top is a sphinx which traditionally is considered to represent your higher self, or in some traditions your holy guardian angel, which can also be equated to your personal daemon. Underneath we have Hermanubis, if the personal daemon is our guide in this life then this figure is our guide in the afterlife, we have now the above and below that we hear so much about; and finally the snake, Hekate, sitting at counter point, the mediator of both realms.

> *I call upon Hekate, Mistress of Life; pour forth your whirling emanations and life generating light to strengthen me as I labour around this cycle of life.*

11 – Justice – They say that justice is blind, and many modern images portray her with a blindfold, the purpose of this is to show that she is impartial, objective, not influenced by fame, politics or money, Justice ensures that each person receives fairly what they are due. This is the Hekate written about by Plutarch who resides on the moon and metes out justice to daemonic souls.

Justice sits red robed and impartial holding a sword in one hand and scales in the other; much like the Hierophant and the High Priestess. However, the Hekate as Hierophant has no veil for she is seated solely in the here and now, the Material world; and the Hekate as High Priestess sit with a Veil of Pomegranates representing her liminal nature between the material world and the aetherial, the unmanifest realm of the soul or the underworld if you will; and finally as justice she sits with a red veil behind her a representation of her liminal nature between the Aetherial and the Empyrean realms; for according to Plutarch, souls do not stay in the realm of Persephone and Hades forever, they remain long enough to shed the *'mind'* they possessed in the material world after which they must pass through the gulf of Hekate and be judged, those who are worthy may enter the Elysian fields or the Empyrean realm and unification with deity if you will. But those who are not, make recompense for their misdeeds.

> *I call upon Hekate, Leader of the worlds, and the gateway between the realms, judge me wisely so that I may be twice born and transcendent.*

12 - The Hanged Man – Sometimes you can feel strung up metaphorically against your will, and sometimes it has to be a conscious decision, something that you do willingly. The Norse God Odin hung for nine days to gain the knowledge of the runes, it was a profound initiatory experience, but he had to remain passive and not struggle or fight against the inevitable for this transformation to take place. This is the epiphany of Hekate, the time when the sun stands still in its path, the moon is hidden and even the world loses it stability.

We see a young man inverted and suspended on a Tau cross, his head is glowing with a supernatural light, he is reminiscent of the youth Iakkhos who accompanied by the Goddess Hekate leads the dark shrouded Mystai on the road to Eleusis. The Tau cross itself is a symbol of the crossroad that Hekate is so famous for; the hanged man's face is passive, he is aware that he is to remain suspended until it is revealed which route he is destined to take, and once that happens then change is not far behind.

I call upon Hekate of Eleusis, companion of the Mystai, initiate me into your secrets and show me the road less taken.

13 – Death – From death springs forth rebirth, both of the body and of the soul, the fool as a seeker of Hekate's mysteries has reached a point where change and transformation need to occur before he can move forward, he has chosen to become one of Hekate's hoard, a marginal in society so that he can develop his spiritual existence. It is in this aspect we see Hekate as the Orphic Goddess Melinoe, a spectre'd form who travels with the terrors of the night.

A skeletal figure dressed entirely in black armour sits astride a snow white horse, so like the description of Melinoe herself, who was said to be partly black and partly white because of the influence of Pluto's dark nature and also Jove's bright one. Before this figure and its noble steed we see a man of the cloth knelt in prayer and supplication, beside him a maiden and child also kneel as if in surrender and below the horse itself is the figure of a king lain as if trampled; this reminds us that nobody regardless of their birth and circumstance can escape this process of transformation if they wish to learn and grow. Fear is often the biggest limitation to this growth and the Orphics called upon Melinoe to dispel *'the soul's mad fears'*, so we may have to do the same and surrender ourselves to the process.

I call upon the night wandering Hekate, infernal Queen; dispel from me that which prevents me from the transformation and rebirth of my ego.

14 – Temperance - A card of balance and harmony, we are reminded that our spiritual journey with Hekate is an alchemical process; like the magician of old who strove to turn base metal to gold; we must blend and combine the base matter which is our physical form and the mundane world around us in an attempt to find the formula that will facilitate us becoming Hekate in a state of henosis. This is the world soul described by Plato, a blending of three pure elements, called the being, the different and the same, or as Eusebius puts it, white, black and red combined.

We see an angel, red wings spread wide, upon his brow is the symbol of the sun, he is fire and air, two of the four basic elements, and he stands one foot on the earth and the other in the water representing the other two elements we know so well. Despite this unusual stance he is completely focused on pouring water from one chalice to another; this whole scene reminds us that Hekate came into being as the world soul as the result of blending these fundamental building blocks of the universe, each in its own very specific proportion and that our path requires us to concentrate equally upon this process.

> *I call upon three formed Hekate, black white and red; reveal to me the sacred ratios so I may achieve union with your divine nature.*

15 – The Devil – If the fool does not learn the lessons of temperance he may fall into the extremes of the material world which from a spiritual perspective is just illusion. The devil is our own foolish nature, our obsessions and lack of balance being the greatest adversary we will ever face when learning the mysteries of Hekate. The devil is Hekate as Physis named in the *Chaldean Oracles*, the theurgists cautioned that her nature was to persuade the unsuspecting and ill prepared that the daemon dogs who accompany her are pure of intent.

In this card we see a Baphomet-style figure crouching upon a cube, bound to which are the lovers; but he is missing the words *solve et coagula* written upon his arms which reminds us that the alchemical lessons of temperance can be forgotten. The devil is the rotting Goddess, the Hekate that Crowley describes as malicious and wholly of hell. Working with Hekate has a price and failing to keep up your side of the bargain can result in the evocation of this side of Hekate, and this is why the Chaldean theurgists warned against evoking this aspect, saying *'her name is like fate'*. After all at the end of the day possibly the worst fate we can receive is that we get what we deserve, is it not?

> *I call upon Hekate the enemy of mankind, leader of the dogs, deceive me not along my path for my intent is pure and my oaths are true.*

16 - The Tower – In the *Old Testament*, men attempted to build a tower so high that they could reach God himself, for their arrogance the tower was destroyed and man lost the gift of a common tongue, man was forced to overcome communication barriers before he could progress any further. To some extents the Tower card tells this story, for when it is struck by lightning it is destroyed and you have to start again with a different perspective. A perspective that is more spiritual and less material. This is Hekate of the Tower as described by Pausanias and also the Chaldean Hekate, one that is dressed in armour of light.

We see the tower, crowned; although the crown is toppling and the tower is burning; figures fall from the tower, one apparently also wearing a crown although it also resembles a jester's hat. The figures have obviously forgotten the purpose of the tower, and have taken residence in their earthly grandeur, they have forgotten that Hekate emits fiery rays of light and unmindful of this they have been struck by her weapons which the Chaldeans claimed were of three barbed strength. Their tower will fall, but Hekate is capable of ensuring great creativity even in the face of destruction for should her lighting strike, you may still perceive her mysteries in the unearthly light.

> *I call upon Hekate wielder of the noetic fire; reveal yourself to me in dazzling light, so that I may concentrate on the lessons you teach.*

17 - The Star – The last two cards have been severe, they are lessons of initiation, trials you must overcome to prepare yourself to take the next stage of your journey with Hekate. The star is the light at the end of the tunnel, the glimmer of hope and success, of the end of the dark night of the soul. This is Hekate, daughter of the starry night; she is also the conflation of Hekate and Rhea which the Chaldeans understood to be the creative force and the font of all divine knowledge.

We see a naked maiden with golden hair bending beside a pool of water, she reminds us once more of the bright coiffered Hekate from the early trump cards when the fool was setting out upon his journey, hope and expectation of the road ahead foremost upon his mind. Above the maiden's head is a bright star surrounded by seven smaller stars which are the classical planets and in each hand the maiden holds jugs from which water gushes forth, one into the lake the other onto the land forming a small stream, the large star is the source of life and the jugs represent the font which was believed to have poured forth from the Rhea/Hekate conflation, the result of which was the generation of power and life.

> *I call upon Hekate first of all in power; pour forth your blessing upon me and be the source of my inspiration and magick.*

18 - The Moon – Just as the star guided the fool from his dark night of the soul, so too can the moon illuminate the way, but the moon casts a different kind of light, shadowed, often morphing objects that are normally non-threatening into objects of pure terror. We dream under the light of the moon and in those dreams we can learn many things if we trust our intuition. This is Hekate not only in her aspect of Selene and Diana; bull horned and riding her silver chariot across the sky, but also the night wandering bringer of dreams, both good and bad many of which can be a gift from the Goddess herself and we can learn from them if we take the time to notice.

The moon itself obviously takes centre stage on this card, although it is apparently full, it has been crafted in such a way that all the phases of her cycles are hinted at. Four phases one for each of the four faces of Hekate. From the moon descend flecks of light, they look like little flames and they resemble the Hebrew letter Yod, the creative principal of divinity, the *'hand of God'*. But what exactly are these flames; they are the oracular daemons who according to Proclus transmit messages to and from the lunar sphere and Hekate. Upon the ground stand two animals entranced by the moon, one of which is obviously a domestic dog whilst the other more feral almost wolf like, both entranced and howling at the moon. The domestic dog appears oblivious that his companion could quite easily make a meal of him; perhaps it is the lunar light that has united them their differences hidden. These dogs remind us of the hounds so often depicted with Hekate and sacred to her, and sometimes used in sacrifice, they are our docile and ferocious natures and they need to be united for us to function completely.

> *I call upon Hekate, bull horned queen, lover of dogs; send down your ferrymen by your blessed light and bring me dreams of knowledge and understanding.*

19 - The Sun – The order of the universe is such that inevitably after the night comes day, after the moon rides her chariot down into the underworld, so the sun comes coursing across the sky; the fool takes comfort in this and feels a sense of balance, all of a sudden the world becomes clear and ordered and the shadows take their proper form. This is the Hekate of Apuleius' *Golden Ass*, for although she appears to Lucius by the moonlight she is Isis-Hekate, a solar deity, all knowing, life giving and all encompassing.

The sun shines benevolently down upon the scene depicted in this card, sun flowers stretch towards the sun and the whole atmosphere is of fertility and abundance, it is on days like this that you can feel like you are capable of conquering the whole world. In the foreground sits a small child, naked, astride a white horse; the Chaldean epiphany of Hekate specifically states that if you call upon her you will perceive a child upon the back of a swift horse, it is a sign that she is with you and success is assured.

> *I call upon Hekate sovereign Queen, child of primordial time; shine down upon me and grant me success in all my endeavours.*

20 – Judgement – The Judgement card is about spiritual redemption and an awakening to the mysteries, the fool with the aid of Hekate has travelled through the material realms in cards one through seven, he has mastered the universal laws she has chosen to show him in cards eight through to fourteen; and now he is reaching the end of the spiritual journey and is ready to be reborn. This is the Hekate that Hippolytus tries to demonise, the Hekate who is capable of resurrection and wanders amongst the tombs of the dead, which accompanies Persephone back from the underworld, and is the maiden Iphigenia who rather than dying as a sacrifice became transformed into Hekate.

We see bodies rising from their tombs, arms outstretched in praise to the angel with flaming hair blowing a trumpet in the clouds above, the souls are naked, new born as children, their resurrection is almost complete, like Iphigenia they have faced death and have been transformed, touched by the dread Goddess, although dread only to those who are afraid of making this transformation, for those who have been to the underworld and back know that Hekate stands, just as the angel does, with torches aflame ready to call and guide the returning soul.

> *I call upon Hekate companion and guide, guardian of lost souls, sound out the call that heralds the dawn and lead me to a new life*

21 - The Universe – The fool is at the end of this journey, but just like life, the end of one journey is the beginning of the next; life's journeys are circular and they rotate in an infinite loop so whilst we may feel triumphant and should take time to enjoy the happiness that our achievement has given us, we should be mindful that with the next turn of the Iynx wheel we shall be back at the beginning taking another path all over again. This card is wholly and totally Hekate Soteira, the world soul of Chaldean thought.

We see what appears to be a maiden dancing, she holds two torches now, symbols of balance, around her is draped a length of fabric, loosely wrapped, still a sign of her serpentine nature but now it is more akin to the girdle described in the oracles that is purported to ensure the fulfilment of things and she dances in the circular wreath of the victor's laurels with seem to confirm this aspect of her. Around the laurels are various images, the bull showing her lunar nature and her connection with Selene, the lion representing her prophetic nature through trance and her connection with the God Bacchus, the eagle shows her aspects that conflated with Artemis and finally the maid she once was, showing that she is all these things at once and more.

> *I call upon Hekate Soteira, world soul, mistress of the universe; crown me with the victor's laurels so that I may celebrate how far I have come and how far I have yet to go.*

DAILY TAROT MEDITATION

Sit comfortably, as with the skrying exercises beware of sitting cross legged on the floor unaided, unless you are very experienced at sitting for any length of time, just use a decent straight backed chair that allows your feet to sit flat on the ground so that there isn't too much pressure on the backs of your thighs. One of the advantages of a straight backed chair is the back support it can offer which should stop you slumping forward and rounding your back, which should also reduce the amount of discomfort experienced when doing this kind of work on a regular basis.

Sort through your deck and remove the twenty two Major Arcana cards, do not order them in any particular fashion, in fact make sure you shuffle them well. Draw a card from the top of the deck. Look at it, think about what the imagery means to you, and compare this to the notes given above. Spend some time studying it until you can close your eyes and visualise the card in reasonable detail, don't worry, this doesn't have to be perfect, it will get better as time goes on.

Imagine that this card is a large windowed door and that the scene on the card is the landscape outside; imagine yourself getting up from your seated position and stepping through the door and into the picture, as you do this call upon Hekate to show you what you need to learn about this aspect of her nature and possibly even your own. As with skrying do not try and process the information in real time, imagine you are a human video camera, faithfully recording events unfolding in front of you. The only exception to this rule is when interaction is required, it may happen from time to time, although probably not as often as you would think and when it does happen seriously consider testing the entity you come across as described earlier. Even if you think it is Hekate herself, she's fairly good at not taking offense at this kind of thing, and as somebody I know once said, paranoid magicians live longer.

Once you feel you have achieved all that you can during this session, and remember little and often is nearly always the best option, either turn back the way you came, until you reach the card/window again, through it you should visualise yourself sitting, step through and back into your body. Or on the odd rare occasion you may find or feel that is not possible to take the return journey, don't panic, stop and visualise the card in front of you once you have it firmly in your mind imagine the image dissolving in front of you and revealing the image of you seated on the other side, then proceed as above. This isn't an ideal scenario, so only use this latter technique if you absolutely have to.

Take some time to *'come back'*, take a few good deep breaths, rub your hands on your thighs or together and then slowly open your eyes,

RITUAL DIVINATION USING THE CARDS

It is always prudent to perform some kind of divination prior to performing ritual; this should be considered as fundamental a part of the process as evoking the Goddess herself. This type of magickal work can influence dates, times and ritual content, and not to be ignored either, the possibility of that really kick arse ritual you just came up with being a complete pile of bull which should be resigned to the cosmic dustbin of rituals which never should have been performed.

These readings won't necessarily tell you what is going to happen, but may indicate outside influences, that had not been previously considered, a good analogy is, that it is the magickal equivalent of a weather forecast, if it says cloudy with a good chance of rain, you don't go out without an umbrella now do you?

If you do not already practise some form of ritual divination, use the meanings given in the section entitled *Using the Tarot to understand aspects of Hekate* and draw a card a day or so prior to each ritual you wish to perform and note the meaning, you may then like to use the meditation technique we have discussed to clarify any details that seem obscure to you.

So for example, you may want to petition Hekate for help regarding a forth coming driving test, you draw the Tower card, this would infer that you are perhaps unwise to perform the rite in the manner you planned as it is for purely selfish and arrogant reasons, a rethink is in order or it may all go horribly wrong. However, once you have made some appropriate adjustments to the rite, you draw another card and this time it is the Sun which would most definitely infer that success is guaranteed and you should go ahead with the ritual.

Remember you should note all this work down in your journal, patterns can often be distinguished when you review written journals.

DIVINATION DICE

"To consult the God you pray in front of the statue, and then take the dice and throw four on the table"[54]

Divination by dice appears to have been a relatively common practise, Pausanias mentions it in his guide to Greece, and the *Greek Magical Papyri* contains a partial example of an oracle using Dice and the Homeric Texts of the *Iliad* and the *Odyssey*. The manner in which the oracle most commonly worked was as follows, a querent would pray to the Gods to provide an answer to their question, after which they would take up the dice which were described as being made from sheep's knuckle bones, the combination of numbers displayed on the dice once cast would then correlate to a specific phase or previously uttered divine oracle.

This form of divination, like the tarot is a technical form of divination, it is a skill that can be learnt rather than being wholly divinely inspired and as such it is a more earthy form of practise; this does not mean that it does not have any value it is a suitable form of divination for rituals that focus on the element of Earth. However, the results, much like in ancient times can be very obscure and do require pondering upon.

Documented examples of these dice oracles often involved four or five dice, however the combinations this would provide are too lengthy to list. Below is an oracle that was created by performing bibliomancy over the three day period which makes up dark moon.

THE ORACLE OF HER SACRED FIRES

It is probably best at this stage to provide some background information regarding the oracle I have provided for you to practise with. In late 2009 I was approached by Sorita d'Este to contribute to an anthology of essays being published about the Goddess Hekate, entitled *Hekate: Her Sacred Fires*.[55] It had over fifty contributors from every inhabited continent on the globe, representing between them many different magical and spiritual traditions.

From *Hekate: Her Sacred Fires* sprang many other project; including amongst them *The Rite of Her Sacred Fires* (a worldwide ritual), and *The Covenant of Hekate* (www.hekatecovenant.com) which hopefully in time will grow into a wonderful collaboration of like minded souls. Additionally

---

[54] Description of Greece Vol 1.7, Pausianas, C2nd CE.
[55] Hekate: Her Sacred Fires, Sorita d'Este (editor), Avalonia, 2010

several of the contributors have gone on to work on further projects this current volume by myself included.

The power of that written collaboration between the contributors of *Hekate: Her Sacred Fires* still progresses onwards here. Originally I had intended to include my own oracle based upon the works of Ovid, Apollonius of Rhodes, Hesiod and others, but a quiet voice in my head said that I should create something contemporary based upon the work in the anthology instead.

This would then more adequately represent a Goddess who operates as strongly in the 21st century as she did two millennia ago. The result of that is the *Oracle of Her Sacred Fires* which follows and which draws on the writings brought together in the book which inspired it. I would like to thank all the contributors for their work, through which they have inspired and created such an unique work of dedication to the Goddess Hekate.

Starting with The Oracle of Her Sacred Fires

Once you have used the oracle provided for a while, you may like to create a dice oracle of your own, for example, you might like to collate all the historical references to Hekate that you can find. Another possibility is to use texts such as Ovid's *Metamorphoses*, Virgil's *Aeneid* and Apollonius of Rhodes' *Argonautica*; all of which are texts that feature Hekate or priestesses of Hekate as key characters.

Choose the text you wish to use (if there is more than one, you may like to number them, throw a dice to randomise the texts).

Calling upon Hekate stating your purpose close your eyes and fan the page edges with your thumb stopping when your instinct tells you.

Still keeping your eyes shut, open the book and place your finger on the page, open your eyes and note the sentence.

If you use six sided dice (although specialist game shops do different dice) then you will need to perform this act two hundred and sixteen times allotting a dice combination to each sentence. This is quite physically and mentally exhausting, however once done it is a very personal oracle that will serve you well for a long time to come.

PRACTICAL EXERCISE – PERFORMING A DICE ORACLE

Using three six sided dice, throw the dice whilst focusing upon the question you wish to have answered calling upon Hekate in her aspect of Hekate Chthonia, note the numbers of the dice, reading them from left to right as they land, then using the oracles provided in the next section look up the three figure combination. So for example you may wish to divine if the next new moon is a suitable time to perform a certain type of devotional ritual, the dice thrown are 1-3-3 which correlates in the table to:

> *"Invoke Hekate in her role as protector of travellers when you embark on your journey [Amelia Ounsted – A Goddess for all Seasons]"*.

You can of course take a number of meanings from this, and it will be your responsibility to work out the finer meaning, but it would infer that yes, the rite could be performed on the next new moon but either, a) you should invoke Hekate before setting out to your ritual working area to avert possible mishap; or b) Hekate Enodia (of the ways) should be invoked as part of the rite, for she will guide you in your coming spiritual journey.

Write both the question and the answer in your journal, as previously stated, the oracle may initially seem obscure to you, if this is the case (which is very likely) spend some time each morning and evening contemplating the response, note any thoughts and feelings that come to you. Also when the oracle becomes apparent note the date and time this occurred and the manner in which it happened.

If clarification is needed it is possible to throw again a second or third time, but I would not advise any more than that, these oracles are not as specific as using Tarot for example and too many throws could confuse the situation.

1	1	1	"I explored the mysteries of the Seven Wandering Stars I invoked the God Dionysus" *[Sorita d'Este, Before We Begin...]*
1	1	2	"I stood up from my kneeling pose, still shaking from the experience but I felt lighter" *[Tina Georgitsis, Illuminating the Path]*
1	1	3	"Hekate speaks to us each and every day, and bids us to see her signs in the mundane reality of our lives" *[Tim Furlow, A Sacred Life]*
1	1	4	"I found some quite astonishing things which explained my accidental interest" *[Georgi Mishev, Threskeia]*
1	1	5	"The strangest things may happen, but she never fails to impress me" *[Yuri Robbers, Ancient Rites Modern Times]*
1	1	6	"Central to the emotional triggers and painful adjustments in the shattering of my ego" *[Orryelle Defenestrate-Bascule, Beyond the Immediate]*
1	2	1	"All of these fail, due to their proponents' oversimplification and to the incredible complexity" *[Trystn M. Branwynn, The Hekatine Strain]*
1	2	2	"Every woman who has ever lived is also my Daughter for what are you if not star stuff" *[Tinnekke Bebout, The Call]*
1	2	3	"For you the work is done, travel to the next destination, I am very proud of you" *[Andrea Salgado Reyes, Following her Moons]*
1	2	4	"But I had a mission to fulfil and it was not my time to go and survive I did" *[Paul Harry Barron, Suffer to Learn]*
1	2	5	"Maybe things don't need to be clearly defined in every aspect of their being" *[Brian Andrews, Twin Torches]*
1	2	6	"It is a natural instinct to seek kindred souls, I also started looking for people who thought in a similar way" *[Georgi Mishev, Threskeia]*
1	3	1	"However in spite of the negative press from these two major occultists, Hekate's worship grew" *[Sorita d'Este, The Hekate Chronicles]*

1	3	2	"Thus we waited contentedly, steadfast on our path" *[Catamara Rosarium, The Heart of Hekate]*
1	3	3	"Invoke Hekate in her role as protector of travellers when you embark on your journey" *[Amelia Ounsted, A Goddess for all Seasons]*
1	3	4	"Her ironic laughter is for all those who, due to ignorance, imagine they can elude spiritual evolution" *[Jade Sol Luna, Goddess of Supreme Consciousness]*
1	3	5	"I spoke, I saw the faces of some of the women present and several women whom I didn't know yet" *[Andrea Salgado Reyes, Following her Moons]*
1	3	6	"She unlocked the door, opened it before me and encouraged me to pass through the door" *[Tina Georgitsis, Illuminating the Path]*
1	4	1	"Harmony occurs where all contradictions are dissolved as Truth" *[Shani Oates, Paean to Hekate]*
1	4	2	"It is my experience that it often helps, and never hurts to put serious effort into any magical work" *[Yuri Robbers, Ancient Rites Modern Times]*
1	4	3	"There was not a day that went passed where I did not ache, physically, mentally" *[Amber-Rose, Tattered Shards]*
1	4	4	"There was a short-circuit somewhere and maybe it was the Goddess herself" *[Paul Harry Barron, Suffer to Learn]*
1	4	5	"I am the flame that burns ever on; All things in the end shall come to me." *[Madre Van Der Merwe, The Fortunes of Hekate]*
1	4	6	"We must also not limit ourselves to thinking about people" *[Kay Gillard, Healing the Soul]*
1	5	1	"The hearts of her devotees, her many manifestations expressed through such forms" *[Sorita d'Este, The Hekate Chronicles]*
1	5	2	"Crossroads have long served both therapeutic practitioners and magical artists on a metaphorical and metaphysical level" *[Katherine Sutherland, At the Crossroads]*
1	5	3	"Understanding would happen as a consequence of experience rather than book learning" *[Tara Sanchez, One Two Three]*
1	5	4	"Something would always be provided, as long as I performed the work that she wishes me to follow" *[Mark Alan Smith, Baptism of Fire]*
1	5	5	"I would look a sight, lying on my back in the middle of nowhere clapping my hands at irregular intervals" *[John Canard, From Heaven to Earth]*
1	5	6	"The Labrys reminds me to listen to the Gods, not just Hekate, very carefully" *[Morgana Sythove, Sacrifices Will be Made]*
1	6	1	"It has the potential to become an extremely mantic experience" *[Shay Skepevski, Hekate's Sacred Lunacy]*
1	6	2	"Fertility and transformation as symbolised by the sexual act as it is about the act itself" *[Amelia Ounsted, A Goddess for all Seasons]*
1	6	3	"By the mysteries of the deep, by the flames of Banal, by the power of the east" *[Ebenezer Sibly, A New and Complete Illustration of the Occult Sciences]*

1	6	4	"The crossing of a road that sees all elements in space and time" *[Catamara Rosarium, The Heart of Hekate]*
1	6	5	"According to the legend, She came in the form of a beautiful maiden to two warriors on the prairie" *[Tim Furlow, A Sacred Life]*
1	6	6	"You traverse all Beginnings, and all ways lead to You" *[Shani Oates, Paean to Hekate]*
2	1	1	"But by the guiding light of the flaming torches of the Goddess Hekate herself" *[Sorita d'Este, Before we Begin...]*
2	1	2	"Physical manifestations of Hecate and Lucifer, that is up until the point they conjoined within my soul" *[Mark Alan Smith, Baptism of Fire]*
2	1	3	"Alas at the end of many months and much thought" *[Dorn Simon-Sinnott, An Illuminating Presence]*
2	1	4	"Axis and its royal couple are one and the same. She is the altar of sacrifice, while he is the sacrifice upon it" *[Trystn M. Branwynn, The Hekatine Strain]*
2	1	5	"And feel the serpents writhe beneath your feet, You who art Mistress of all those beasts" *[Lezley Forster, She is I and I am She]*
2	1	6	"These pivotal moments in our lives provide opportunities for us to become" *[Diane M. Champigny, A Rite for Hekate]*
2	2	1	"Persephone, who dost detest heaven and thy mother" *[Lucan, Pharsalia]*
2	2	2	"Sacrifice part of the truth in order to tell a better story, or tell a story in a better way" *[Yuri Robbers, Ancient Rites Modern Times]*
2	2	3	"But a balance of the scientific/operative realm and the intuitive/theurgic realm are key" *[Raven Digitalis, Personalizing the Mystery]*
2	2	4	"Of course I could ask her, but I prefer to call on her when there is great need" *[Thomas Starr, Hekate's Angels]*
2	2	5	"And I experienced and learned so much more. Without her I would be stagnant" *[Henrik Holmdahl, She Leads the Way]*
2	2	6	"Fear may also be found in the multitude of inner doubts that we hold about ourselves" *[Connia Silver, Shining her Light on Fear]*
2	3	1	"The last piece of the puzzle before I learned about her existence came to me" *[Henrik Holmdahl, She Leads the Way]*
2	3	2	"If proper respect is given to this powerful Goddess, one can petition her help" *[Raven Digitalis, Personalizing the Mystery]*
2	3	3	"Then, at right angles, the three attendants were in a row holding bread" *[Andrea Salgado Reyes, Following her Moons]*
2	3	4	"By the mirkness [darkness] of the moon - let mirkness remain" *[David Rankine, Hekate wears Tartan]*
2	3	5	"To me, the snake symbolises an innate freedom and liberation" *[Vikki Bramshaw, Swaying with the Serpent]*
2	3	6	"I could see and feel what the possessing spirit could, almost in a 'second-hand' way" *[Soror Basilisk, The One who waits at the Crossroads]*

2	4	1	"The Mystery Cults of the ancient world were initiatory traditions" *[Sorita d'Este, The Hekate Chronicles]*
2	4	2	"Turned to for guidance when I was crying out for a new direction in my life" *[Kay Gillard, Healing the Soul]*
2	4	3	"The moon was full, and hung low in the sky, making the white stones silvery blue" *[Morgana Sythove, Sacrifices will be Made]*
2	4	4	"Is this empowering? Is it even aligned to a person's true personality type?" *[Raven Digitalis, Personalizing the Mystery]*
2	4	5	"I had assumed that everything I observed on the astral had also taken place on the physical" *[Soror Basilisk, The One who waits at the Crossroads]*
2	4	6	"This initial find led me on a crooked path of research to the Capon Tree" *[David Rankine, Hekate wears Tartan]*
2	5	1	"The place was full of power despite not having been used as a place of Pagan worship for 1600 years" *[Morgana Sythove, Sacrifices will be Made]*
2	5	2	"The symbolism we find when exploring a non ordinary reality can be fascinating" *[Kay Gillard, Healing the Soul]*
2	5	3	"We believe in the existence of a spiritual reality bound up with the physical one" *[Georgi Mishev, Threskeia]*
2	5	4	"In a way, I become a crossroads; the physical and the astral converging to allow something truly magickal" *[Soror Basilisk, The One who waits at the Crossroads]*
2	5	5	"And never has he taken anything that she was given in the Age of Titans, the Gods of yore" *[Yuri Robbers, Ancient Rites Modern Times]*
2	5	6	"While the higher emotions - love, trust, loyalty - we understand as products of our divine awareness" *[Trystn M. Branwynn, The Hekatine Strain]*
2	6	1	"I find working with trance one of the most powerful ways of getting in touch" *[Vikki Bramshaw, Swaying with the Serpent]*
2	6	2	"The key of working with two shadows is that here are two lights" *[Brian Andrews, Twin Torches]*
2	6	3	"And with dire madness he may scare any maiden from her bower" *[Yuri Robbers, Ancient Rites Modern Times]*
2	6	4	"Nobody wants painful changes to happen - we would rather they all changed in a nice and pleasant manner" *[Paul Harry Barron, Suffer to Learn]*
2	6	5	"When I was skrying in the ashes I got a bit of a shock! Isis had three heads!" *[Madre Ven Der Merwe, The Fortunes of Hekate]*
2	6	6	"An Oracle. I was getting images from her mind - a woman of the 1930's" *[Soror Basilisk, The One who waits at the Crossroads]*
3	1	1	"If the patient is attended by fears, terrors and madnesses in the night" *[Hippocrates, On the Sacred Disease]*
3	1	2	"There was a power in working with people that you trusted and an energy that exists" *[Lezley Forster, She is I and I am She]*

3	1	3	"By the time her decision was definite it was too late to find someone else to take the part" *[Orryelle Defenestrate-Bascule, Beyond the Immediate]*
3	1	4	"A feature that was not planned was the mask she wears" *[Emily Carding, Painting Hekate]*
3	1	5	"Divination, death and dying, wealth and abundance" *[Raven Digitalis, Personalizing the Mystery]*
3	1	6	"Your eyes have fear at the sight of me, but your soul trusts me" *[Naza Cogo, Dark Night of the Soul]*
3	2	1	"Her Sacred fires are also the fires which burn, and have burned in the past or will burn in future" *[Sorita d'Este, Before We Begin...]*
3	2	2	"Instead I have to carefully look at things from more than one angle" *[Brian Andrews, Twin Torches]*
3	2	3	"This might be a time to work with animal headed Hekate or with the energies of the animals" *[Amelia Ounsted, A Goddess for all Seasons]*
3	2	4	"Striding through all of this, through mythology and history, with his hammer in hand" *[Trystn M. Branwynn, The Hekatine Strain]*
3	2	5	"Purposely fall on the floor in front of me, taking a myriad of other sacred items" *[Dorn Simon-Sinnott, An Illuminating Presence]*
3	2	6	"There were of course many mutual friends within the dissolving partnership" *[Orryelle Defenestrate-Bascule, Beyond the Immediate]*
3	3	1	"But once under the aegis of Hekate, these and other issues bubble to the surface and need to be dealt with" *[Paul Harry Barron, Suffer to Learn]*
3	3	2	"The otherworld is directly linked with fairies and elves, who are implied as her servants" *[David Rankine, Hekate Wears Tartan]*
3	3	3	"We do not consider soul force as something which is fully present within our bodies at all time" *[Kay Gillard, Healing the Soul]*
3	3	4	"I heard a voice like a thunderclap, and saw a terrible woman approaching" *[Lucian, Philopseudes]*
3	3	5	"Was this the price I would have to pay? To live in this world of darkness" *[Naza Cogo, Dark Night of the Soul]*
3	3	6	"And I will always honour her through my deeds and thoughts" *[Madre Ven Der Merwe, The Fortunes of Hekate]*
3	4	1	"The lessons she will teach are wholly dependent upon your own particular view point" *[Tara Sanchez, One Two Three]*
3	4	2	"I now had a powerful friend in the form of the local library" *[Hansa, Om Hekate Krim]*
3	4	3	"I was fighting with my own soul, my own heartbeat" *[Naza Cogo, Dark Night of the Soul]*
3	4	4	"What unites us is the common concept and belief in the Goddess as an all-embracing force" *[Georgi Mishev, Threskeia]*
3	4	5	"It is through these liminal times and places that gateways to the otherworlds are sought" *[Richard A. Derks, A Druid & Hekate]*

3	4	6	"The serpents of the paths sweep and clean, open new ways, seek new paths" *[Andrea Salgado Reyes, Following her Moons]*
3	5	1	"There are numerous meteor showers through the year, most of which are not easily visible" *[John Canard, From Heaven to Earth]*
3	5	2	"The last minute preparations began the day before with the purchase of ingredients" *[Andrea Salgado Reyes, Following her Moons]*
3	5	3	"Like Ixion, I was tied, albeit initially unawares, to a wheel spinning round" *[Tara Sanchez, One Two Three]*
3	5	4	"The priests noticed how I always hung around the temple whenever I could, having hurried my chores" *[Hansa, Om Hekate Krim]*
3	5	5	"I would have visions of the world around me dissolving into pure energy" *[Shay Skepevski, Hekate's Sacred Lunacy]*
3	5	6	"I urge you not to fear her even in the form of battle, death and destruction" *[Amber-Rose, Tattered Shards]*
3	6	1	"I confronted one of my greatest fears and now I grow into a more powerful witch" *[Shay Skepevski, Hekate's Sacred Lunacy]*
3	6	2	"Food for the restless dead" *[Sorita d'Este, The Hekate Chronicles]*
3	6	3	"Senses to the point that I could function more efficiently, though I left driving until much later in the day" *[Mark Alan Smith, Baptism of Fire]*
3	6	4	"I spent the remainder of that day quietly counting the hours" *[Tara Sanchez, One Two Three]*
3	6	5	"Another old belief is that a shooting star represents a birth" *[John Canard, From Heaven to Earth]*
3	6	6	"Marked by the unusually strong flaring up of the central candle when each touched the altar" *[Andrea Salgado Reyes, Following her Moons]*
4	1	1	"Until she arms him, this is to say, until she admits him into the world of mature awareness" *[Trystn M. Branwynn, The Hekatine Strain]*
4	1	2	"Now that connection has been re-established, she will be by my side to guide and advise" *[Soror Basilisk, The One who waits at the Crossroads]*
4	1	3	"Hecate brought many teachers to aid in our work" *[Mark Alan Smith, Baptism of Fire]*
4	1	4	"And on the darkest night we say that he has died. Yet this is not a linear path" *[Amelia Ounsted, A Goddess for all Seasons]*
4	1	5	"Showed her genitals to Demeter to make her laugh and drink the sacred drink kykeon" *[Sorita d'Este, The Hekate Chronicles]*
4	1	6	"Delving to the depths of darkness to re-emerge into the light cleansed, renewed" *[Dorn Simon-Sinnott, An Illuminating Presence]*
4	2	1	"As Christianity became the dominant religion in Europe, Hekate's presence was less obvious" *[Sorita d'Este, The Hekate Chronicles]*

4	2	2	"Not a conscious one, but that evening was a turning point, a milestone for me" *[Jen Ricci, Ravens]*
4	2	3	"Encourage you in the unique opportunity to save yourself through transformation" *[Connia Silver, Shining her Light on Fear]*
4	2	4	"And firmly oriented towards obtaining spiritual freedom at all costs" *[Jade Sol Luna, Goddess of Supreme Consciousness]*
4	2	5	"We converge and begin our journey to the ritual site. It's dusk and the air is dense with fog" *[Catamara Rosarium, The Heart of Hekate]*
4	2	6	"Light in my darkness and the darkness which nourishes the light" *[Andrea Salgado Reyes, Following her Moons]*
4	3	1	"So what if anything has changed about the Torchbearing Goddess of the Mysteries?" *[Sorita d'Este, The Hekate Chronicles]*
4	3	2	"In all honesty, I do not expect anyone to be able to relate to this" *[Amber-Rose, Tattered Shards]*
4	3	3	"The soul through wisdom, from the bonds of ignorance into the Liberty of Light" *[Shani Oates, Paean to Hekate]*
4	3	4	"Mother is a very intuitive person and she was very right, of course I could use it" *[Henrik Holmdahl, She Leads the Way]*
4	3	5	"She stands firmly in the present, while viewing the past and the future at the same time" *[Connia Silver, Shining her Light on Fear]*
4	3	6	"At this time when our quest for balance within ourselves can require some painful soul searching" *[Amelia Ounsted, A Goddess for all Seasons]*
4	4	1	"Revealed herein are three fundamental deific attributes" *[Shani Oates, Paean to Hekate]*
4	4	2	"Suddenly, the unmistakable feeling of being watched. It was very very strong" *[Jen Ricci, Ravens]*
4	4	3	"Hear now the words of the Dark Maiden, who was from the beginning and is for Eternity" *[Shay Skepevski, Hekate's Sacred Lunacy]*
4	4	4	"None have been more profound than that of my darkest hour" *[Amber-Rose, Tattered Shards]*
4	4	5	"A wide variety of practises surrounding the different facets of Meter" *[Vikki Bramshaw, Swaying with the Serpent]*
4	4	6	"It was of a rough stone. Two ears - life size - had been carved into it" *[Morgana Sythove, Sacrifices will be Made]*
4	5	1	"Hekate enthroned and in a pose more often associated with the Great Mother" *[Sorita d'Este, Timeline]*
4	5	2	"Biting stinging gusts blow against me, hindering every step, hours seem to pass" *[Shani Oates, Paean to Hekate]*
4	5	3	"Important that this not be rushed by feelings of self-consciousness and embarrassment" *[Diane M. Champigny, A Rite for Hekate]*

4	5	4	"Also cover some general information about these festivals, so as to make clear Her relevance to them" *[Amelia Ounsted, A Goddess for all Seasons]*
4	5	5	"She had an optimistic nature, which was reflected in the happiness and laughter" *[Hansa, Om Hekate Krim]*
4	5	6	"Never failing me and making me appreciate that to do my will I do not need the personalities" *[Michael Ellis, Untouched]*
4	6	1	"I had no choice, but to bite the bullet and get on with it, gritting my teeth as I did so" *[Paul Harry Barron, Suffer to Learn]*
4	6	2	"Then she said to me, go back to your beginning, so I shall" *[Tara Sanchez, One Two Three]*
4	6	3	"One can be sure that things may not happen as we envisage them, and, probably not to our own moral timescale" *[Shani Oates, Paean to Hekate]*
4	6	4	"I instinctively concluded that each order of angels should rather belong to a triad in itself" *[Thomas Starr, Hekate's Angels]*
4	6	5	"Was horrendous. I felt trapped, like the life was being crushed from me" *[Mark Alan Smith, Baptism of Fire]*
4	6	6	"In true Fortune style I gathered the woods to make the Fire of Azrael" *[Madre Ven Der Merwe, The Fortunes of Hekate]*
5	1	1	"Noise was bringing forth all manner of bizarre visions from my unconscious mind" *[Thomas Starr, Hekate's Angels]*
5	1	2	"Red is most obviously the colour of blood and fire, and hence is connected to the qualities of action" *[Emily Carding, Painting Hekate]*
5	1	3	"It was in love and, I admit, the thirst for more knowledge and power that I did just that" *[Mark Alan Smith, Baptism of Fire]*
5	1	4	"Dance with me you say, And so I dance" *[Shani Oates, Paean to Hekate]*
5	1	5	"Work has come to a grinding halt or I am unsure of where to go next! Life interferes" *[Lezley Forster, She is I and I am She]*
5	1	6	"She has become wise with age and time and can see portents of the future" *[Diane M. Champigny, A Rite for Hekate]*
5	2	1	"Every night, at midnight I ran a high temperature and as a result of it I hallucinated" *[Georgi Mishev, Threskeia]*
5	2	2	"Lucid dreaming and dream analysis is extremely useful, especially when experiencing" *[Connia Silver, Shining her Light on Fear]*
5	2	3	"Part of this time of sleep and darkness has already been covered in Yule" *[Amelia Ounsted, A Goddess for all Seasons]*
5	2	4	"Beneath the layers of colour we reach through the keyholes, we again return to the stars" *[Emily Carding, Painting Hekate]*
5	2	5	"The hound, we find operating in a number of different ways" *[Trystn M. Branwynn, The Hekatine Strain]*

5	2	6	"That my trust of Hecate was implicit. It was only because our relationship was so intense" *[Mark Alan Smith, Baptism of Fire]*
5	3	1	"She loves a pure heart: she might not be one for hugs and fluffiness" *[Jen Ricci, Ravens]*
5	3	2	"Of course there are others one could use, but this harsher time of the year works better for me" *[John Canard, From Heaven to Earth]*
5	3	3	"I had no better resources and not in a position to argue" *[Amber-Rose, Tattered Shards]*
5	3	4	"New hope to guide your way, even the smallest spark will show up brilliantly in pitch blackness" *[Connia Silver, Shining her Light on Fear]*
5	3	5	"Found myself in a spontaneous swirling dance with a man of heavier build than myself" *[Orryelle Defenestrate-Bascule, Beyond the Immediate]*
5	3	6	"Herbs should be ground into a very fine dust powder and then sifted" *[Henrik Holmdahl, She Leads the Way]*
5	4	1	"Of witchcraft, and many other attempts at being alternative, with varied levels of success" *[Petra Schollem, Days for the Dead, and Living]*
5	4	2	"It was as if this oath was somehow meant to strengthen our connection, and let the true work begin" *[Richard A. Derks, A Druid & Hekate]*
5	4	3	"Now it is the time of night that the graves all gaping wide, Everyone lets forth his sprite" *[William Shakespeare, A Midsummer Night's Dream]*
5	4	4	"They say eyes are the mirror into your soul, while mine writhed in torment" *[Amber-Rose, Tattered Shards]*
5	4	5	"These run from the toxic and Saturnine, to the fertile and Venusian" *[Trystn M. Branwynn, The Hekatine Strain]*
5	4	6	"Asked if human remains had been found there he replied yes, but that the deceased was first burnt" *[Morgana Sythove, Sacrifices will be Made]*
5	5	1	"Nevertheless it formed an excellent foundation around which I could create" *[Thomas Starr, Hekate's Angels]*
5	5	2	"Who has captivated not only my heart but my intellect too, setting me alight with flames" *[Michael Ellis, Untouched]*
5	5	3	"But had it not been for the authority and strong-headedness of our high priestess" *[Paul Harry Barron, Suffer to Learn]*
5	5	4	"This knowledge was delivered with compassion, but reinforced with glimpses" *[Mark Alan Smith, Baptism of Fire]*
5	5	5	"Ten rows of steps leading to the stone paved road. The temple, encircled with five rows of steps" *[Morgana Sythove, Sacrifices will be Made]*
5	5	6	"Discover images of Her in unexpected places, books (or other information) would present themselves unsolicited" *[Diane M. Champigny, A Rite for Hekate]*
5	6	1	"Left Hermes, with eight-rayed star above his head" *[Sorita d'Este, Timeline]*

5	6	2	"The fourth participant connecting with the energies formed from the Hektarion" *[Catamara Rosarium, The Heart of Hekate]*
5	6	3	"Interest in tribal rites of passage, and it was only a matter of time before my first tattoos and piercings" *[Tim Furlow, A Sacred Life]*
5	6	4	"Next I pondered who was the double-wanded one who would assume my throne and place" *[Michael Ellis, Untouched]*
5	6	5	"Pour the white wine into a large silver bowl and allow the vessel to sit beneath the light of the full moon" *[Shay Skepevski, Hekate's Sacred Lunacy]*
5	6	6	"Without symbols the mind is blind. Without love, the heart is dead" *[Shani Oates, Paean to Hekate]*
6	1	1	"Derived from the ritual cry Iakkhe, made by his priests when they bore the twin torches" *[Sorita d'Este, The Hekate Chronicles]*
6	1	2	"When from that equipoise of light and dark the days become shorter and the nights longer" *[Orryelle Defenestrate-Bascule, Beyond the Immediate]*
6	1	3	"It's really pretty perfect, a place where Earth, Sea and Sky meet" *[Richard A. Derks, A Druid & Hekate]*
6	1	4	"The simultaneous existence of these three processes within the creation" *[Jade Sol Luna, Goddess of Supreme Consciousness]*
6	1	5	"No fakery, no frippery, not tools, no games, she is here and forever will be" *[Lezley Forster, She is I and I am She]*
6	1	6	"Even though she is standing off to one side apparently inactive, it is actually an example and encouragement" *[Brian Andrews, Twin Torches]*
6	2	1	"There is separation, but there is simultaneous unity" *[Raven Digitalis, Personalizing the Mystery]*
6	2	2	"None may forbid it, your influence will reach two sisters and three sons of Hekate" *[Andrea Salgado Reyes, Following her Moons]*
6	2	3	"Hence it is that when the unstable soul advances by the path of Saturn" *[Dion Fortune, Psychic Self Defence]*
6	2	4	"Of course my ordeals were far from over. My rite had given me hope for change" *[Orryelle Defenestrate-Bascule, Beyond the Immediate]*
6	2	5	"This fringe of a cloak that Delphis lost I will shred now and cast into the cruel flames" *[Yuri Robbers, Ancient Rites Modern Times]*
6	2	6	"Levels of consciousness, both awake and sleep, sane and mad, conscious and unconscious" *[Shay Skepevski, Hekate's Sacred Lunacy]*
6	3	1	"So devour me, Fate, I surrender to your whims! Even to your apparent caprice, For why struggle" *[Orryelle Defenestrate-Bascule, Beyond the Immediate]*
6	3	2	"I also feel that it's important to be open to what Hekate has to teach you Herself" *[Amelia Ounsted, A Goddess for all Seasons]*
6	3	3	"Oh Daughters of Hekate! Each betrayal brings its punishment" *[Andrea Salgado Reyes, Following her Moons]*

6	3	4	"Snakes are decisive, and strike with intent and precision" *[Vikki Bramshaw, Swaying with the Serpent]*
6	3	5	"A declaration to our great mother requesting her presence on this night" *[Catamara Rosarium, The Heart of Hekate]*
6	3	6	"While today the term lunatic is commonly used in a negative sense" *[Shay Skepevski, Hekate's Sacred Lunacy]*
6	4	1	"Now it's not often that I hear voices in my sleep as such, but when I do I have learned to sit up" *[Richard A. Derks, A Druid & Hekate]*
6	4	2	"The cave stone on the side of the shrine is an idea from a dream" *[Henrik Holmdahl, She Leads the Way]*
6	4	3	"The obvious tool to use during these times is a piece of meteorite" *[John Canard, From Heaven to Earth]*
6	4	4	"That image struck hard in my mind. I had missed quite a few cycles" *[Amber-Rose, Tattered Shards]*
6	4	5	"By then I instinctively understood what it was I was meant to do" *[Petra Schollem, Days for the Dead , and Living]*
6	4	6	"The very choice to walk along one particular path over another is the very essence of the crossroads" *[Raven Digitalis, Personalizing the Mystery]*
6	5	1	"Offerings were a standard part of the veneration of the Gods" *[Sorita d'Este, The Hekate Chronicles]*
6	5	2	"For some years it suited me just fine, because it had what I needed" *[Ekaterina Ilieva, The Red Veil]*
6	5	3	"In fact the intensity of the black energy now increased. I could see Hecate" *[Mark Alan Smith, Baptism of Fire]*
6	5	4	"But try as I might it really was not working for me" *[Richard A. Derks, A Druid & Hekate]*
6	5	5	"A journey of great sadness at times and one of great joy when the task has been completed" *[Petra Schollem, Days for the Dead, and Living]*
6	5	6	"He did not actually create or cause evil, but instead pointed out the evil that mankind perpetrates" *[Paul Harry Barron, Suffer to Learn]*
6	6	1	"We can be forced to re-evaluate truths we have previously subscribed to in the past" *[Katherine Sutherland, At the Crossroads]*
6	6	2	"A fiery being which moved between the worlds as an intermediary or a messenger" *[Vikki Bramshaw, Swaying with the Serpent]*
6	6	3	"When one is at a crossroads, Hekate is there to show the options" *[Soror Basilisk, The One who waits at the Crossroads]*
6	6	4	"And if you would have received me, it would have been most pleasant" *[Yuri Robbers, Ancient Rites Modern Times]*
6	6	5	"A feeling of relief, then soul moves towards portal" *[Andrea Salgado Reyes, Following her Moons]*
6	6	6	"Would represent the Cosmic order and be the power behind the Gods" *[Sorita d'Este, The Hekate Chronicles]*

DREAM INCUBATION

"To sleep, perchance to dream. Ay, there's the rub! For in that sleep of death what dreams may come"[56]

The power of dreams was not something to be underestimated in the ancient world, for in the realms of sleep, the dreamer could be visited by Gods and daemons; they could be cured or cursed, and even influenced by other human beings who practised magickal arts. Famous sanctuaries were constructed purely for the purpose of sleeping in sacred space in the hopes that the God to which the sanctuary was dedicated would aid the sleepers in whatever it was that they sought, healing being quite a popular request.

The *Greek Magical Papyri* is littered with spells which professed to everything from making the victim die as a result of the dreams that were sent, to making a desirable female fall in love with the magician performing the spell. The ritual of the cat evoking Hekate to aid in sending the ghost of a poor dead moggie to terrify unsuspecting dreamers in their sleep[57] is a particularly relevant example considering the deity involved, although any readers with a faint heart or a squeamish nature might not want to follow this reference up too closely for it involved performing some rather vomit inducing operations to the cat before the spell could be manifested.

Now whilst of course no sane person could advocate the torturing and murder of an innocent animal to satisfy the need to give an undesirable a bit of a fright, the art of dream sending and dream incubation can be practised and learnt through far less nefarious routes. This is why so many beginners' books stress the importance of a dream journal, although sadly so few explain exactly what the purpose of this journal actually is. As already stated dream work can be broadly divided into incubation (receiving) and propagation (sending) and during the work with the elemental Hekate you will have, hopefully, already experienced dream incubation.

The techniques for the two are explained individually below with practical exercises for you to experiment with.

DREAM INCUBATION

Using the timetable given in the introduction to this chapter choose a suitable night on which to perform this rite, any day which states *'all day'* will do.

---

[56] Hamlet, Shakespeare, c. 1600 CE.
[57] PGM III.1–164.

Eat lightly in the evening; avoid tobacco, caffeine, alcohol and any other potentially altering substance, and yes that even includes chocolate, sorry folks.

Take a bath or shower and cleanse yourself thoroughly, and make sure that if you sleep in night wear these are clean, change the bedding as well.

Write on a slip of paper the question you want answered, or the ailment you wish relieved (health and safety warning – dream incubation is no substitute for a visit to a qualified medical practitioner) and either burn it whilst saying a prayer to Hekate, or place it under your pillow again with a prayer.

Even if you live with a partner, attempt to retire to bed alone even if it is by just a half an hour or so; and under no circumstances participate in sexual activity.

Record all dreams in your journal, you will quickly come to recognise when you receive *'one of those'* dreams for there is a certain something about them, a depth that isn't easily describable, however; do not be tempted to act too rashly, the Gods are just as capable of throwing you a curve ball and sending you duff information, Zeus was particularly famous for sending people on wild goose chases.

DREAM PROJECTION

This isn't as bizarre and farfetched as you would think, how many times have you told a friend or a loved one of the terrible night you had because of surreal dreams, for them to say that they too had experienced dreams that would make Salvador Dali proud? Multiple family members having nightmares on the same night? Or even friends calling to check you are alright because they had a dream about you? This is often the result of unconscious dream projection from one person propagating to their nearest and dearest. The knack is to make the projection conscious, but how?

You could of course summon up ghosts of the dead, or evoke daemons that are inclined to perform such tasks; however Hekate has a track history in this particular kind of work. Aeschylus writes, *"thou art frighten of a spectre beheld in sleep and joined the revel-rout of Hekate"*.[58] It was a common theme during the classical period that nightmares were the result of a visitation from Hekate, some physicians even believed that illnesses were caused as a result of her manifesting in a patient's dreams. So it seems fairly obvious that the best thing to do is cut out the middle man and go to her direct.

This exercise works best with a partner, there is a grey area around the ethics of doing this with an unwilling recipient so best to work with someone who doesn't mind having a bit of subconscious rummaging going on, trust is a key issue here, don't abuse it. Also if possible work with a partner who is either very good at dream recall or keeps a dream diary, there is no point in

---

[58] Fragment 249, Aeschylus, C5th BCE.

working with one of those souls who always sleep like a log and rarely remember a thing the next morning; believe it or not people like this do exist, the author's husband is one such individual.

As before observe ritual and physical purity, bathe, change sheets, put on fresh nightwear etc.

Decide in advance what it is you want to project, start simply at first, shapes, sounds, even smells, then build up, try images of the recipient's favourite film star, covers of favourite books, the list is endless, eventually once you feel you have mastered this technique you can then focus on such subject as healing, and actual messages.

Prior to retiring spend a little while alone, breathing deeply and focusing your mind on the task ahead; the tetrahedron meditation is good for this.

Once calm and grounded, take three deep breaths, and then perform the gesture for vision.

Light a candle on your altar and place a photo of the person you wish to receive in front of it, and focus on the flame, summon Hekate using a mantra or other prayer, there is an example mantra in the section entitled *Hymns and Invocations*, use this if you wish until you are comfortable writing your own.

When you feel that Hekate has heard you, stop chanting and visualise the image you wish to project whilst staring at the photo.

When the image eventually fades, gently ask Hekate to send this image, thank her for her presence and extinguish the flame.

Discuss the night's events with the person in question, take notes and record as normal.

THE TEMPLE OF HEKATE

"The true rituals take place in the mind and the subtle, invisible realms"[59]

A temple is a permanent space set aside for religious and magickal practise, nearly every major culture (with a few notable exceptions), both past and present have built these sacred places, as a sign of devotion to their Gods and the Egyptians, Greeks and Romans were no exception.

In certain cultures it appears that orientation of the temple was quite important which can be readily seen with such monuments as Stonehenge and New Grange where the sun at the solstices falls in very specific locations, many of the ancient churches in Britain are set in an east-west orientation, which some believe is proof that the Druid faith was subsumed into Christianity, and very curiously a recent study of ancient temples built in Sicily by Greek colonists shows an overwhelming propensity for east-west positioning, with a very interesting exception, that of the Temple of Hekate at Selinus, which was built facing west, which would allow for sunlight to enter the sanctum at sunset and moonlight to cascade through the colonnades at moonset rather than the sun flooding through at sunrise, which would almost infer a liminal and mostly nocturnal purpose.

Bryn Celli Ddu, a Neolithic site aligned to the Summer Solstice

---

[59] Practical Techniques of Modern Magic, Green, 1993.

Many temples followed a similar theme as far as structure and organisation was concerned, the general populace was given access to the ritual areas in the grounds and sometimes the outer sanctum, whilst the inner sanctum or *'holy of holies'* sometimes called the Adyton was preserved for initiates and priesthood only.

ESTABLISHING TEMPLE SPACE

If you are lucky enough, either alone or as a group to have a permanent place in which to gather and perform your rites it would be beneficial to create a permanent working area or temple, a loft space, attic, even a garage can be used for such an endeavour and the creation of the temple is an excellent focus for your work with Hekate and creates and important nexus for a group. Considering appropriate correspondences and collecting and decorating it with sympathetic items, regularly performing ritual within it, even sleeping in it can create a level of energy and a bond that no ad hoc circle casting will ever quite match.

Many practitioners if their circumstances allow have permanent dedicated space be it within their homes or local environment; for its permanency in the physical realms has a knock on effect in the otherworld too, and if you create such an area you may find that your divination and oracular work is more profound within this space or that the energy raised is more tangible, think about an ancient site you have visited (and if you haven't visited one, get out there and do), there is often a certain *'something'*, a buzz, shivers down your spine, a metallic taste in the back of your mouth. Megalithic sites are a really good example of this, millennia's worth of people visiting them for one purpose or other all storing their energies in the landscape around, and there they sit thrumming away like an advert for a well known battery, sadly now with no way of expending it for long gone are the days when anybody knew how such temples were used and their accumulated energies directed.

One of the other benefits of a working temple besides the residual energy effect is that it can be consecrated and activated in such a way that it may have a guardian or guardians in situ allowing it to remain indefinitely *'open'*. Then a lot of work can be performed such as meditation, skrying and other forms of divination with little or no extra protection required, leaving the circle as a tool only used for specific purposes such as invocation and evocation. This standpoint of course does receive mixed reviews but it may just be because for so many people it would be horrendously difficult to keep this area entirely sacred and once you sully it with the mundane and profane you are in essence back to square one with the task of making it pure again; however, if you take the view that every conscious act is an act of magick then even day to day actions, if performed thoughtfully, should not affect the overall structure of the temple in the other worlds, it is where carelessness happens that the problem arises.

For those that cannot create a permanent area, either alone or in a group, there is a way to create a temple that everyone can access regardless, and that is through by-passing the mundane reality completely, it too has to be carefully constructed, more so in fact, for its inherent protection will need to be greater to stop others from stumbling upon it. But with work and dedication a temple can be constructed, consecrated and activated directly upon the astral realms which only those with the correct keys can access, and it is this we shall be exploring next. The method of consecration and activation are essentially the same for both physical and astral temples, so to avoid repetition these techniques are discussed only in the next section but feel free to use them when constructing a physical temple.

THE ASTRAL PLANE

> *"The Astral Plane, which lies between the material and the spiritual"*[60]

Although there are nuances in opinion, normally relating to a particular magickal order or school of thought, the general consensus is that the astral plane (or realm) exists at a higher vibrational or energetic frequency to our own mundane material world. Within each of us we possess a body of energy, which we can fashion more or less to be identical to our own mundane flesh, if we so wish, and with which we can travel to and interact with this higher realm of being.

This body of energy has been given a number of names including body of light, astral body and in certain witchcraft traditions the title of fetch, although the latter may cause some interesting discussion depending upon whom you speak to and which combination of occultists are currently sitting in the corner arguing the toss.

Whilst every living thing in the material realm has a marker or body on the astral realm, the astral realm does not exactly mimic the material world, however it is here, especially for those who are not so gifted in clairvoyance and clairaudience in an everyday capacity, that we can interact with the denizens of the unseen realms, and primarily in our case the Lady Hekate. It is even possible to meet and interact with others who follow her ways whose diverse geographical locations might otherwise preclude you from normally doing so.

THE ASTRAL TEMPLE OF HEKATE

Astral projection and mental projection are two different practises and experiences, the former can take a great deal of practise, possibly even a lifetime to achieve proficiently, the latter less so; and can be practised daily with minimum effort almost from day one. In reality many people who claim to be working on the astral are doing so only in a mental capacity, that is not to say that their work is any less valid and the technique of mental projection is the preliminary stages for developing a full projection, but for

---

[60] Liber A.B.A (Book Four), Crowley, 1992.

anybody beginning their journey into the world of occult practises, to hear more experienced practitioners tell of their wonderful temple, the rituals they perform and the entities they meet there, can make the whole thing seem just a little bit daunting.

Firstly we have to answer some basic questions: What is an astral temple, what do you do whilst you are there, what are the benefits of using an astral temple over a physical real world ritual space?

To answer these questions, it is probably best to start at the beginning; and apologies to the more experienced practitioners who feel like they are being taught to suck eggs, but even the most experienced of us can sometimes benefit from a different perspective or a refresher of concepts already learnt, if you've got this far you're probably here for the duration so you may as well settle in for the ride.

THE ASTRAL TEMPLE AND WHAT YOU DO IN IT

As we have stated above everything on the material realm has a shadow or echo, for want of better words, residing in the astral realms. That does not of course mean that everything in the astral occurs in the material, but for now that is a little bit by the by. If we create a permanent temple structure in the material world then it will have an equal shadow on the astral, repeated use will strengthen that shadow and make the temple more permanent.

An astral temple is exactly the same as one built in the here and now, only its construction takes place entirely on the astral plane, a practitioner or group (for it can be created by a group mind especially if they have a close bond) has entered this world and constructed it piece by piece. Obviously you do not have to literally build it brick by brick, but it must be crafted lovingly in fine detail nonetheless and the more you work with it the more tangible it will become.

As to its function, well you can do pretty much anything in it you can imagine, ritual, meditation, spell work, summoning of entities and invoking and evoking of deity. Some prefer to perform their evocatory work within an astral temple as it adds a layer of abstraction and therefore you aren't physically summoning anything into your material environs, which of course can be a concern especially for those that have children and other family members to consider.

BUILDING THE TEMPLE OF HEKATE

To start with you will need a strong idea of what you wish your temple to be like, in the practical exercises there is a temple visualisation of a bare bones temple to help you if you are lost, it draws upon imagery we have covered over the lifetime of this book and will provide you with the materials to start building your own astral temple. It has been designed in such a way that there is already some level of security already inbuilt, for it requires the four words or symbols that were revealed to you during the early elemental meditations, failure to provide them, should stop opportunist prying eyes gaining access.

Otherwise if you wish to make it entirely your own from the start; then if you have even a small talent in drawing you may like to sketch how you wish your temple to look like both internally and externally, gathering samples of material, colours swatches and images from books and magazines may also aid you in gaining a real feel for how your finished temple will manifest. As with the temple provided you will need to design some form of security, be it passwords or gestures that you and/or your group will need to use to gain access; even creating some kind of thought-form to serve as guardian can also be useful but not totally necessary for the activation ritual that has been provided is fairly powerful in its own right.

PRACTICAL EXERCISE

Once you feel you are ready to begin construction understand that just like Rome your temple will not be built in a day and although you can effectively *'will'* a wall or a roof or a fantastic marble altar into existence, your temple will be more robust and complete and *'real'* the more you work on it. If you are building your own temple from the ground up, you may like to write a description of the temple which you will memorise over a period of a few days or spend some time each day studying the designs and artwork you have created, otherwise use the template below and learn it by heart before you start the first *'construction'* session.

Prior to each session it is wise, unless you are already working in an active material temple, to perform a banishing and cast a circle, this may seem a little tedious initially as these sessions may at first only last a few minutes but as time goes by and the bond with your temple becomes stronger you may find you can spend longer and longer working on and in your temple, it is also wise to perform a banishing after each session also just to make sure you don't bring any hitchhikers back with you.

A warning is required here, do not fall into the trap of spending your entire magickal career as an astral interior designer though, constantly tweaking this and that, and then never actually using the space you have created for its intended purpose. This may well be a particular problem when a group is working on the same mental image, one person always finding a reason to keep making changes. This is a difficult situation but if anybody ever tells you that a magickal working group is a democracy then they are lying, in the best case scenario you will be more likely working in an oligarchy and worst an autocracy, there will always be people who take control and take charge and do the decision making, that is just human nature, and in truth most people are happy to let this happen thus abdicating a level of their own personal responsibility and unless the person who is refusing to progress is actually the one with the bigger boots; it's time to utilise these personalities within the group to ensure progression.

It may be that the person fiddling around and dragging their heels is either not ready to make this step; or alternatively is having great difficulty tuning into the group mind, an issue which you will need to address in some way or another. This might be suggesting that the person spends a period working individually on their own personal temple, which they can then spend as much time as they like tweaking, before they return to what should be by then a very real and operational group temple, or possibly one to one training with different group members in turn thus hopefully helping that person grasp the different aspects of the group mind before being totally overwhelmed by the whole. Of course in some situations it may eventually require a gentle suggestion that they continue their journey onwards with the Goddess alone.

But that is sort of a little off the subject, as this book is not intended to be a primer on the pastoral skills required to run a coven or magickal order; so once you (or the majority of your group) are confident that you have more than a passing feel for your temple and can visualise it consistently for a reasonable period of time without deviation then it is time to consecrate it, activate and jolly well use it.

TEMPLE VISUALISATION

Imagine yourself standing just in front of a row of marble temple columns, each deeply grooved and in the shadows just beyond are two large wooden doors, heavy and inlaid with iron studs. You step forward and try to push the doors open with both your hands but they seem heavy and require some force to move them.

To open them you need to visualise words or symbols you discovered whilst doing your elemental meditation, inscribed on the doors of the temple, each glowing faintly in the pale moonlight that is cascading through the gaps between the columns in silvery shafts. As these words appear, the doors start to move and you discover that they will now swing both easily and smoothly inwards until with a deep thud they hit the stoppers on the interior.

Stepping through into the chamber, you realise that the room is shadowy but not dark, as it is lit by a vast array of candles, hanging from both the fantastic circular cast iron chandelier above the centre of the room and adorning the low altar in the centre.

The floor is cool on your bare feet, looking down you notice that it is a highly polished black and white chequered marble floor, each tile measuring roughly thirty centimetres on a side. You notice that one of the flags appears to be inlaid with a strip approximately two centimetres in width, of reddish brown stone, Jasper perhaps, looking more closely you notice that an adjacent flag also contains some of this stone too, taking in the whole scene it becomes quickly apparent that this inlay creates a perfect circle surrounding the central altar and it is approximately eighteen foot in diameter.

Stepping across this line of red, into the circle, the doors closely almost noiselessly behind you, with just a gentle whoosh of air alerting you to what has happened. Confident now that you are safe and secure from intruders you make your way across to the low altar to examine it. Kneeling down and running your hands along the surface of the top of the altar you sense what you initially think is a fault line running directly down the centre of the altar, but closer inspection reveals that in fact it is made of two stone cubes pushed together, each cube is about half a metre on a side, creating a rectangular top surface.

When it is time to leave, you stand and turn and walk towards the doors, as you cross the threshold of the circle you feel a resistance, like you are being held back, you visualise the words or symbols from the elemental meditation and this resistance diminishes, the doors start to swing open and you walk forward and out through the doors and back into the material world the doors of the temple closing firmly behind you.

Make at least a half a dozen visits to the basic temple before adding any additional detail, you may find that with each trip, things reveal themselves to you, and things that remain constant over a number of trips should be noted and incorporated into your overall vision, if you feel uncertain or uncomfortable about anything that presents itself, perform a simple banishing, draw a banishing pentagram for example and project it at whatever object is causing disquiet, if it waivers in anyway perform a full banishing ritual before progressing onwards.

Try and spend at least ten minutes a day or longer if possible, over a period of at least a lunar month constructing your temple, very quickly you will realise that you will be able to slip in and out with relative ease and towards the end of this period you may wish to experiment with accessing the temple outside of a circle or physical temple and note if there are any differences or difficulties in making this change; after all one of the nice things about an astral temple is it is accessible anytime and anywhere, so you need to be comfortable with doing this in case you ever feel a need to access it quickly.

In the final week of these exercises, take time to learn the activation ritual by heart, if you are working with a group you may wish to adapt it so that the entire group may have a part to play in the role thus strengthening the bond for everyone. Also you will need to write a dedicational hymn to Hekate as part of the rite if possible consider writing this in the temple, as part of your daily visit; contemplate a line or two of the hymn each time and take it away with you from the temple and note it in your journal.

As you will have noticed no doubt the security measures in place are the requirement of the personal words or symbols to give access and egress from the temple, it is at this time nothing more than a simple thought- form that provides a locking mechanism. However you may wish to expand on this thought-form, giving it specific tasks, a name and more importantly a shut down program for there may come a day when something happens that requires you to make a quick exit, or has left you sufficiently spaced out that you temporarily forget the necessary words or symbols in which case you can effectively trigger the thought-form into *'fail-safe'* mode, with the doors opening as part of this action.

The best way to program your thought-form temple guardian is to first consider exactly what its purpose will be, right now, if you based your temple on the example above you will have subliminally already started this process because of the requirement to open and shut the temple doors with passwords and the resistive sensation you felt when attempting to leave the circle without visualising them. Is this all you want the thought-form to accomplish or would you like it to do more? Alert you of tampering for example, how would you like that alert to take place, do you want the thought-form to tickle you (or a designated member of the group) behind your left ear, or are you happy that it detain an intruder within your temple walls until you return to deal with it?

You may like to house it in a physical object within the temple environs so as it grows, which it probably will, it will not be immediately obvious to unwanted visitors, and should you wish, you could have a corresponding object in the physical world allowing the guardian to move more readily between the realms. The list is endless, but at least at first, it is better to keep instructions short, sweet and simple. One thing you do need to consider is the lifetime of this guardian; will it remain operative for only as long as the temple is being used? Or the group who created it are still functioning? This is important, bored thought-forms can become a menace, stories of the antics of abandoned thought-forms are pretty common and can be humorous, such as the thought-form that took to flushing the toilet at odd hours of the day and night to gain attention, through to the positively nasty such as a guardian that left to its own devices started terrorising the inhabitants of the house it was situated in and regularly threw things around.

Once you have formulated clear and concise statements regarding form, function, lifespan and shutdown criteria, the next step is to visit your astral temple, sense the already vaguely detectable presence of its energy and call it to coalesce in front of you, it doesn't take fancy words, just will and intent. Draw energy in through your nose so that not only are you breathing air but the very substance of the universe itself and exhale it out through your mouth visualising this energy streaming towards the embryonic entity you are creating, with each exhalation this creature should take on a more solid form within your mind's eye; if you are working as a group you may wish to take it in turns to mould and instruct this little fella. Once the form of the entity is complete you need to program it, recite over and over its purpose, its life span, its shut down protocols, if when you moulded its body your intent was for it to be able to speak, make it recite this information over and over again, tell it where it lives, who it can and cannot take instruction from, and if it helps as you speak imagine a constant stream of ones and zeros flooding from your mouth and into the creatures body filling it up like lines of computer code.

ACTIVATING THE TEMPLE

Once you are confident with the robust nature of both your temple structure and its guardian should you have chosen to create one, you are now ready to dedicate the temple to Hekate, activate it and make it a fully functional sacred space. The following ritual has been designed to do just that, and is based upon a well established ritual known as the *'Opening by Watchtower'* created by the Hermetic Order of the Golden Dawn, you may be wondering why you would want to use such a ritual, and the answer is quite simple, it was based upon fragments of the *Chaldean Oracles* and an excerpt from the *Greek Magical Papyri* and therefore is totally suited to our purpose, why spend a lifetime re-inventing the wheel? However if that is what floats your boat, study the ritual provided, understand its function and go ahead and create something new, better if you can, life is about growth and innovation after all.

THE RITUAL OF OPENING

You will need to decorate the altar of the temple appropriately for the ritual, possibilities are dressing it with material representing the elemental colours, which are yellow, red, blue and green; or perhaps colours traditionally associated with Hekate, such as black, white, red and grey or yellow. Place upon the centre a suitable effigy of Hekate; whether a representation of something you already have in the physical realm, or one that you can imagine that adequately represents how Hekate appears to you, is entirely your decision. A censer is also an idea, for burning incense, if you can mentally construct it to be one of the orbed ones on a chain which can be swung more the better, but that is mainly for those that like a little bit of bells, smells and whistles and general high magick prancing around, it isn't absolutely necessary. You may also wish to decorate the altar with symbols of a particular tradition you work in and with other items that relate to Hekate, the point being that the Goddess to whom the temple is being dedicated is adequately represented and honoured.

Take time to light candles, ignite incense blocks, add incense to the coals, organise offering and libations etc. If working as a group it may be best to decide who is responsible for these tasks before hand and provide them with a bell to ring in the physical plane as well as the astral to indicate when everything is prepared. It is also worth bearing in mind that some people take longer to adjust into the astral even when only projecting mentally and this may need to be practised a number of times prior to performing the rite fully so a quiet period may need to be incorporated once the preparations are completed. This is also where learning the ritual by heart and your extended practise in skrying and visualisation will come into its own for as a group, it may be possible to verbalise the spoken parts in the physical whilst maintaining the mental link, thus enabling individuals to know exactly where everyone is should they find they are starting to zone out. You will have to think carefully about this though, for some people find the act of stimulating the physical body can completely return them to the material world.

The other option is for each person to memorise the ritual in its entirety, internally performing their roles as necessary but working at their own pace, of course somebody is now going to say, how does that work, and won't it all be out of synch? Well from a material and linear time perspective, yes it would, however on the astral realms time is far from linear and with will and intent each individual action will be brought into phase with the others. This of course is not a problem when working alone. From here on in the ritual has been written as if it was being performed by a single person, groups will of course as discussed need to divide it up as they see fit, preferably playing to people's strengths rather than egos.

Lifting the censer and starting at the east progress around the circle in a clockwise manner, swinging the censer as you go, proclaiming *HEKAS, HEKAS, ESTE BIBELOI*, which in English effectively means; '*Away, away, O Ye Profane ones.*'

Move to the south quarter, raise your arms in the gesture of praise and hold it for 3 heart beats, bring your arms down and out in front of you and perform the gesture of thumbs again for 3 heart beats, then finally drop your left arm down to your side and open out your right hand in the gesture of summoning.

Say:

> *And when after all the phantoms have vanished, thou shalt see that holy and formless fire, that fire which darts and flashes through the hidden depths of the universe, hear thou the voice of fire.*
>
> *Hekate Phosphoros*
> *Offspring of the starry skies*
> *Torchbearer*
> *Whirring forth from the aether*
> *Cloaked in a fountain of flame*
> *Hekate Phosphoros*
> *Horse headed queen*
> *Light bringer, fire breather*
> *Come forth to bless and protect this space which I/We have created in your honour.*

From the south walk a circuit around the circle marked on the floor passing south and onto the western quarter, raise your arms in the gesture of praise and hold it for 3 heart beats, bring your arms down and out in front of you and perform the gesture of thumbs again for 3 heart beats, then finally drop your left arm down to your side and open out your right hand in the gesture of summoning.

Say:

> So therefore first the priest who governeth the works of fire must sprinkle with the lustral water of the resounding sea.
>
> Hekate Enodia
> Goddess of Harbours
> Only begotten
> Wild haired and dancing
> Your arms are decorated with serpentine jewels
> Hekate Enodia
> Serpent headed Nymph
> Granter of favours
> Come forth to bless and protect this space which I/ We have created in your honour

From the west, walk a circuit around the circle marked on the floor, passing both west and north a second time and onto the eastern quarter, raise your arms in the gesture of praise and hold it for 3 heart beats, bring your arms down and out in front of you and perform the gesture of thumbs again for 3 heart beats, then finally drop your left arm down to your side and open out your right hand in the gesture of summoning.

Say:

> Such a fire existeth, extending through the rushing of air, or even a fire formless whence cometh the image of a voice, or even a flashing light, abounding, revolving, whirling forth, crying aloud.
>
> Hekate Propolos
> Bright shining Lady
> Guardian of the night sky
> Chariot riding mistress of the moon
> Whose brow is adorned with the horns of a bull
> Hekate Propolos
> Bull headed dame
> Lover of solitude
> Come forth to bless and protect this space which I/ We have created in your honour.

From the east, walk a circuit around the circle marked on the floor passing east, south and west a second time and onto the northern quarter, raise your arms in the gesture of praise and hold it for 3 heart beats, bring your arms down and out in front of you and perform the gesture of thumbs again for 3 heart beats, then finally drop your left arm down to your side and open out your right hand in the gesture of summoning.

Say:

> *Stoop not down into that darkly splendid world wherein continually lieth a faithless depth and Hades wrapped in gloom, delighting in unintelligible images, precipitous, winding, a black ever rolling abyss, ever espousing a body unluminous, formless and void.*
>
> *Hekate Prytania*
> *Night Wanderer*
> *Invincible Queen*
> *Cave Dwelling Goddess of dark and light*
> *You who are crowned with a circle of Oak*
> *Hekate Prytania*
> *Dog headed maid*
> *Dressed in dusky robes*
> *Come forth to bless and protect this space which I/We have created in your honour.*

* From the north turn clockwise and return to the central altar facing east. Hold your arms up in the gesture of praise for three heartbeats, then perform the gesture of thumbs for three heartbeats and again raise your arms in the gesture of praise.

Say:

> *I evoke ye, ye angels of the celestial spheres whose dwelling is in the Invisible. Ye are the guardians of this sacred space. Keep far removed the evil and the unbalanced. Strengthen and inspire me/us so that I/We may preserve unsullied this abode of the mysteries. Let my sphere be pure and holy so that I/We may enter in and become a partaker of the light divine.*

Slowly and with reverence now walk the circle three times clockwise before returning to the centre.

Say:

> *Great Hekate, Queen of the night, brighter than the day, we dedicate this sacred space in your name, may you grace us with your divine knowledge and grant us the keys to your mysteries.*

Sit in silence for a while, meditate on the energies of the temple and any instructions which Hekate may give you. When you feel ready kneel in front of the central altar and extinguish all but one of the candles which should be left burning at all times (in a physical temple this is of course not possible for safety reasons, but a candle should be lit immediately upon entering the temple space).

Say:

> I now declare this temple duly open.

Try and use the temple as often as possible and at least once every six months or so re-consecrate the space using this rite, it will help keep its protection strong. If for any reason it is necessary to decommission this space, perform the ritual again but after you have finished at * recite the following.

Say:

> Ye angels of the celestial spheres whose dwelling is the Invisible, Guardian of this sacred space I thank you for your attendance in this sacred space, return in peace unto your rightful place.

Say:

> I now declare this temple duly closed.

HYMNS, MANTRAS, EVOCATIONS AND INVOCATIONS

"Heaven and heavenly things take delight in wonderment, worship, praise and service from humans"[61]

Mankind has forever shown their devotion to the Gods through music and dance, art and literature; and the power of the spoken word can be one of the most profound and magickal forms of devotion. Just like music, dance and the ritual gestures we perform there is a level of mystery which cannot be denied, for once spoken words are released out into the aether bound for the other realms never to be reclaimed. The ancient Greeks understood the power of the spoken word, many of their prophecies and epic verses were written in hexameter a poetic form of prose, where lines were written containing six (hex) feet of verse, where a foot was considered to contain a certain number of syllables, as follows:

Foot 1 - 4	One long and two short, or two long
Foot 5	One long and two short
Foot 6	Two long, or one long and one short

We of course do not need to be quite so precise with our devotional orations, after all our modern minds have not been educated in that way, but the care and consideration taken to compose our hymns and prayers should be just as precise in intent. Below are some traditional and modern hymns which can be used within rituals you may want to create, but also for inspiration when writing your own orisons to the Goddess Hekate.

---

[61] Corpus Hermetica. Asclepius C2nd-C3rd CE.

TRADITIONAL HYMNS

Proclus Diadochus' Hymn to Hekate and Janus
(Translation by Yuri Robbers)

Hail, many-named Mother of Gods,
Thy children so fair
Hail, mighty Hekate of Thresholds
And hail also to Thee, Forefather Janus,
Zeus the undefeated
Hail to Thee, Zeus most high!
Create the course of my life in luminous Light
And stack it high with all that is good,
Drive sickness and evil from my limbs.
And when my soul rages with worldly worries,
Free me with soul-stirring rites of purification.
Yes, give me Thy hand I pray
And reveal to me the pathways of divine guidance that I yearn for,
Then I shall gaze upon Thy precious Light
Whither I flee from the evil of our dark origin.
Yes, give me Thy hand I pray,
And when I am weary, let Thy winds carry me to Thy haven of piety.
Hail, many-named mother of Gods,
Thy children so fair
Hail, mighty Hekate of Threshold
And hail also to Thee Forefather Janus,
Zeus the undefeated,
Hail to Thee Zeus, most high.

Sophocles' Hymn to Helios and Hekate
(Translation by Yuri Robbers)

O Master Helios and Sacred Fire
O spear of Hekate of the Crossroads
Which she bears while approaching Olympus
And dwelling on Earth's holy Crossroads
She who is crowned with oak-leaves
And the coils of wild snakes.

CONTEMPORARY HYMNS

Devotional Orison (based upon **Liber Astarte Vel Berylli Sub Figura CLXXV**, by Aleister Crowley)

Oh great and terrible queen, she of the three ways, hear me I beseech you
Grant me your blessings as I prostrate myself before you.

Hear these words as I kneel in obedience; you to whom my central hearth is dedicated,
An oath of fealty I swear, for I am your loyal subject.

Great Mother, you who guides me, protects me, and grants me the grace to grow in the image of my own creation; I honour you as a dedicated daughter.

Oh Mighty Lady, you shine so bright even the stars pale before you, like brilliant torches you light my way. As your humble priestess, I dedicate this rite in worship of you.

My sister, you who knows me better than myself, you who holds the keys to my deepest soul
In trust I give my secrets to your safe keeping.

My dearest friend whom does embrace me often, who accompanies me on paths others will not go
In companionship I share this rite with you.

My dearest love, whose words are like honey on my lips, whose caresses are like whispers on the wind. This rite is an expression of our passion and in perfect love I perform it for you.

Devotional Mantra (based upon **Liber Astarte Vel Berylli Sub Figura CLXXV**)

Observe the fire burns without form; hear the voice that whispers from it;
Behold the Soul, Dark Hekate, Numenic, Harmonic, Chaotic, Chthonic.

Evocation of Hekate Trimorphis

Hear my call, she who is my chosen accomplice
To whose presence this rite is dedicated
I hearken for your dread hounds calling, Dark Lady come hither

Three times three I call as is your right
Three times, for earth and sea and sky
I hearken for your dread hounds calling, Dark Lady come hither

Great Lady I call you, she of many forms
Come forth from the sea
Stand before me with your ravening host
I hearken for your dread hounds calling, Dark Lady come hither
Great Lady I call you, she of the many ways
Come forth from the earth
Stand before me with your ravening host
I hearken for your dread hounds calling, Dark Lady come hither

Great Lady I call you, she of many names
Come forth from the sky
Stand before me with your ravening host
I call you now, Dark Lady come hither

Invocation of the four-formed Hekate

Hekate Prytania
Night Wanderer
Invincible Queen
Cave Dwelling Goddess of dark and light
You who are crowned with a circle of Oak
Hekate Prytania
Dog headed maid
Dressed in dusky robes
I invoke thee

Hekate Phosphoros
Offspring of the starry skies
Torchbearer
Whirring forth from the aether
Cloaked in a fountain of flame
Hekate Phosphoros
Horse headed queen
Light bringer, fire breather
I invoke thee

149

Hekate Enodia
Goddess of Harbours
Only begotten
Wild haired and dancing
Your arms are decorated with serpentine jewels
Hekate Enodia
Serpent headed Nymph
Granter of favours
I invoke thee

Hekate Propolos
Bright shining Lady
Guardian of the night sky
Chariot riding mistress of the moon
Whose brow is adorned with the horns of a bull
Hekate Propolos
Bull headed dame
Lover of solitude
I invoke thee

RITUAL PLANNING AND PERFORMANCE

Whilst freeform ritual can be very liberating and enlightening, this tends to only be effective when working alone or with a group of close knit individuals that already have an established track record of working together. There is nothing more disappointing than a poorly executed ritual, with sheaves of paper and people struggling to read complex instructions by candlelight, normally failing miserably. The whole thing comes across like a poor rehearsal at the local amateur dramatics club, rather than a profound experience of the mysteries.

Having a standard liturgy that can be explained simply, pre-ritual, to any who may not have experienced this way of working before is often the best way to overcome this problem and there is a whole wealth of information available to reconstruct a working procedure. The first thing to do is decide what is important to you as a practitioner or as a group. How the altar is prepared and constructed, purification and preparation of sacred space, ritual structure including how prayers invocations and evocations are to be performed and when, are all issues that need to be considered. This can all be broken down into a number of subsections, some of which will be redundant if you are working alone so adapt as appropriate:

PREPARATIONS:

- What is the purpose of the ritual; is it part of the standard ritual year, or something very specific?
- Which aspect of Hekate will you call upon within this rite?
- Do you wish to evoke other deities alongside Hekate, if so who, and is it appropriate; for example, calling upon Demeter and Poseidon to aid in the healing of a sick horse might seem like a really good idea, but what you might end up with is the Olympian version of Jerry Springer!
- Will you be working in an astral or permanent temple or outside in the local area, if it is the latter, are there any nature spirits or local deities that will need to be acknowledged or even consulted before you go inviting strange Gods into their territory. If there are, and your work is geared toward the environment; protection of the wildlife on a stretch of river bank is a really good example, you need to ask yourself, if it might be more appropriate to be asking for help from the natives before inviting outside contractors in.
- Are you planning on giving certain attendees specific roles, for example who will be responsible for any invocations or evocations? Remember not every person either wants to, or is cut out to take a starring role in ritual, and that has to be taken into

consideration, or you may have very unhappy group members at the end of the rite.

- How many participants will there be within the ritual, what are their experience levels, do any of them have physical considerations which may affect timing and location?
- What materials are required, such as special incenses that need to be made, votive offerings, and ritual tools; and who will provide them?
- Will the ritual need music or other ambient noise?
- Who can be relied upon to be available to prepare the temple or working area beforehand and clear up afterwards?
- If a feast is going to be part of the ritual, who is responsible for the preparations and how are you going to deal with allergies or addictions?

PURIFICATIONS

This book has spent a long time waxing lyrical regarding the importance of ritual purification both of space and person. By now you should be fairly convinced about the necessity of these forms of preparation; so this should of course be observed by both yourself and every member of a group participating in the ritual, there will however be times when additional purifications of both self and possibly particular ritual items will need to be considered.

- Do you wish to provide bathing facilities prior to the ritual?
- Would you prefer to provide some form of font containing consecrated water and purifying herbs, if so which herbs will you use, will you choose them according to planetary correspondences or other association; will they be suitable for use by all the participants?
- Will everybody have access to clean robes? Is it even sensible to wear robes, ritual on deserted hillsides might better be served by wearing warm clean clothes and sensible footwear, can you adequately serve the Gods with hypothermia or a broken ankle?
- Will you incorporate some form of energetic purification to help balance even the most *'airy'* of personalities prior to the rite?
- What embargos will need to be set in place, avoiding alcohol and stimulants at least 24 hours prior to a rite can ensure that people aren't still processing poisons from the night before.

SETTING THE SPACE

The space within your magic circle should be thought out carefully, and the following can be used as a check list to ensure that you have all bases covered.

- Which type of sacred space are you using, circle or temple?
- If you are using a circle where will the altar be positioned?
- Who will cast it?
- What type of altar will you use, chthonic or Olympian?

- How will it be decorated and is the symbolism appropriate for the ritual?
- Who is responsible for setting the altar?

RITUAL STRUCTURE

Tablets found at temple sites, which were in effect book keeping ledgers, have shown us that performed or planned ritual had a prescribed format; Burkert states that a tablet found at Pylos details the list of offerings for the God Poseidon as:

> *"Wheat, Wine, One Bull, Ten Cheeses, One Rams fleece, and Honey"*[62]

By studying other such tablets scholars have been able to ascertain that the order of the items listed in these tablet ledgers have a proscribed format, which, correlates directly to the order in which they were offered to the deity in question within the ritual.

- Preparatory grain offering (corn, wheat, cakes)
- Libation (water and wine)
- Meat offerings (often involving immolation)
- Additional *'bloodless'* offerings (cheeses, animal skins, oils, honey etc.)

You will need to decide which offerings you wish to include and where and for what purpose, the following ritual is an example of a well thought out and planned ritual; it was performed by twenty four people in 2007 with some very surprising results which may well have had a lot to do with the time and the effort all the participants put into the preparation and performance of the rite.

The rite was performed during the Attic month of Boedromion and roughly corresponded with the Greater Mysteries of Demeter and Persephone and were celebrated as such, it was based around information provided by Ginzburg,[63] a prominent scholar in the witch trial manuscripts, who discovered that a group of *'Benandanti witches'* in a remote part of Italy travelled in trance to a sabbat to fight evil, their Goddess had many names but one of them was Hekate.

---

[62] Greek Religion, Burkert, 2004.
[63] The Night Battles, Ginzberg, 1992.

THE NIGHT BATTLE RITUAL

PRE-PLANNING:-
- First Aid Kit
- Lighters
- Torches
- Oil Burners
- Glasses
- Firelighters
- Robes
- Face Paint
- Incense
- Water
- Black unprocessed lamb's wool
- 4 raw racks of lamb
- Mead
- Honey Cakes
- Pebbles
- Musical Instruments

LOCATION:-
Weather permitting outside around a bonfire, failing that inside around a lit fire.

TOOLS REQUIRED:-
- Charcoals should be burning in 4 receptacles inside the circle at the quarter points ready for incense to be burnt, reason; if there is to be a manifestation, the fire will not obscure it for any participants, she has a habit of appearing in smoke.
- Glasses for entire group.
- Mead and honeycomb for the Eucharist.
- Rack of lamb tied with black wool for the offering.
- Drum and horn (and other assorted instruments for the *'armies'*)
- Torches to mark the battlefield
- Pebbles to mark the boundaries

THE SUMMONS:-

The Benandanti were summoned with a drum, it is fair to assume the same happened for the witches, participants to be summoned to ritual by an insistent beating drum.

THE PURIFICATION:-

Priestess: In front of the fire

Herald: Rhythmically beating the drum until all are assembled

Chorus: Enters, forms a circle around the fire, with the judges standing at quarters.

Priestess: Once group assembled, proclaims:-
> *Hekas, Hekas, Este Bibeloi*

Priestess: Silently turns sprinkling bay infused water on the assembled group, proclaiming again:-
> *Hekas, Hekas, Este Bibeloi*

Judges: close into the circle, symbolically *'whip'* the backs of the group, again whilst proclaiming:-
> *Hekas, Hekas Este Bibeloi*

Judges move on, group joins in with the proclamations increasing with fervour, this continues until every member of the group has been purified and a full circle turned, judges return to their positions.

Priestess: Faces the fire again, claps 3 times at which point the judges will walk into the circle through the group and liberally sprinkle incense onto the charcoal. They will back out and join the group in the circle as equally spaced as possible.

ORISON:-

Priestess:
> *Oh great and terrible queen, she of the three ways, hear us we beseech you*
> *That you may grant us these items that are laid before you*

Chorus:
> *Observe the fire burns without form; hear the voice that whispers from it*
> *Behold the Soul, Dark Hekate, Numenic, Harmonic, Chaotic, Chthonic*

Priestess:

Hear these words as I kneel, to you, to whom this central hearth is dedicated, an oath of fealty I swear. These items I bring you as your loyal subject

Chorus:

Observe the fire burns without form; hear the voice that whispers from it
Behold the Soul, Dark Hekate, Numenic, Harmonic, Chaotic, Chthonic

Priestess:

Great Mother, you who guides us, protects us, and grants us the grace to grow in the image of our own creation; I honour you with these offerings as your dedicated daughter.

Chorus:

Observe the fire burns without form; hear the voice that whispers from it
Behold the Soul, Dark Hekate, Numenic, Harmonic, Chaotic, Chthonic

Priestess:

Oh Mighty Lady, you shine so bright even the stars pale before you, like brilliant torches you light our way. As your humble priestess, I dedicate these items in worship of you

Chorus:

Observe the fire burns without form; hear the voice that whispers from it
Behold the Soul, Dark Hekate, Numenic, Harmonic, Chaotic, Chthonic

Priestess:

My sister, you who knows me better than myself, you who holds the keys to my deepest soul. In trust we give these items to your safe keeping

Chorus:

Observe the fire burns without form; hear the voice that whispers from it
Behold the Soul, Dark Hekate, Numenic, Harmonic, Chaotic, Chthonic

Priestess:

My dearest friend whom does embrace me often, who accompanies me on paths others will not go. In companionship we share these items with you

Chorus:

> Observe the fire burns without form; hear the voice that whispers from it
> Behold the Soul, Dark Hekate, Numenic, Harmonic, Chaotic, Chthonic

Priestess:

> My dearest love, whose words are like honey on my lips, whose caresses are like whispers on the wind. These items are an expression of our passion and in perfect love we shall consume you.

EUCHARIST

In silence and solemnity –

Priestess: Hands out the honeycakes
Herald: Hands out the mead

When all have received the sacrament, everyone participates in consuming the body and the blood, a small amount of the *'blood'* should be retained by each participant which will be added to the fire later.

EVOCATION

Priestess:

> Hear my call, she who is our chosen accomplice
> To whose presence this rite is dedicated

Chorus:

> Hearken to your dread hounds calling, turn magic wheel and bring the victors home

Priestess:

> Three times three we call as is your right
> Three times, for earth and sea and sky

Chorus:

> Hearken to your dread hounds calling, turn magic wheel and bring the victors home

Priestess:

> Great Abbess we call you, she of many forms
> Come forth from the sea
> Stand at our head with your ravening host

Chorus:

> Hearken to your dread hounds calling, turn magic wheel and bring the victors home

Priestess:

> Great Abbess we call you, she of the many ways
> Come forth from the earth
> Stand at our head with your ravening host

Chorus:

> Hearken to your dread hounds calling, turn magic wheel and bring the victors home

Priestess:

> Great Abbess we call you, she of many names
> Come forth from the sky
> Stand at our head with your ravening host
> We call you now
> Frau Holle – Abundia – Satia – Hekate

All (three times getting louder):

> Hekate, Hekate, Hekate, bring the victors home

LIBATION AND OFFERING:-

Going anticlockwise, each person in turn takes a lamb chop and places it on the fire, pouring the remainder of their mead as a libation into a receptacle (needs to be something one can carry, a jug perhaps) then turns and walks from the fire area, they must not look back, Priestess is last to leave the area (with the libation receptacle).

PROCESSIONAL TO BATTLE FIELD:-

During the processional, each participant is to utter prayers to Hekate, preferably ad lib.

BOUNDARY/LIMINAL ENERGY RAISING:-

'Judges' place the torches at the 4 quarters

Participants start weaving in a circle, in and out chanting, clapping hands, stamping feet in total abandon.

Malandanti and Benandanti together:

> Black Spirits and white, red spirits and grey, Benandanti, Malandanti going to join the fray (to be repeated over and over until fever pitch).

Herald: Horn is blown and the battle commences.

158

RULES OF ENGAGEMENT FOR THE BATTLE

The Players
- Priestess of Hekate,
- Herald
- Four Keepers of the Mysteries (or Judges, these are participants with physical conditions with exclude them from battle)
- Benandanti
- Malandanti

The field is marked out with boundary stones, large sea washed pebbles, 22x22 paces. The Herald's pace is the measure. The Priestess, Herald and Keepers are outside the field, the Benandanti and Malandanti within it.

At the commencement of battle a horn is sounded by the Herald.

Combatants are *'killed'* either by being put across the boundary and kept from re-entry for a count of 27, or being pinned with both shoulders to the ground for a count of nine within the field.

The Judge's decision is final as to *'death'*.

Every *'death'* within the field entitles the Judge who is nearest to move one boundary stone inwards one pace. Every *'death'* by *'putting out'* is considered a sacrifice to the Goddess and is rewarded by the nearest Judge moving a boundary stone outwards half a pace.

The Battle continues until only one contestant remains within the field. The side to which that one belongs wins and gets to rule the territory of the field as it is at the time of cessation of hostilities. They with the judges of opposite gender repopulate the field reincarnating the *'dead'* by mimicking giving them birth from the edge of the field, the priestess acting as midwife.

RE-BIRTH/CLOSING OF THE RITUAL:-
Dead contestants to line up behind the female judges who act as *'pillars'* holding hands in an arch way much like the children's game *'oranges and lemons'*. They will one by one walk into the archway; hold out their hands to be guided through by the priestess and walk away from the battle field.

Priestess:
> *Pass through the gates from the Elysian Plains back to the house of Demeter and the fields of the earth.*

POST RITUAL:-
Priestess: Will be the last to leave the battle field, the previously collected mead libations will be poured at the base of the torches and the torches extinguished at which point Hekate will be thanked and very politely asked to take her leave.

Hopefully this example will serve to give you an idea of not only the level of planning sometimes necessary to perform a provocative and moving rite, but also how the prayers and evocations in this book can be used to create full, dramatic and meaningful ritual.

APPENDICES

I - HEKATE AND OTHER GODS

> *"Even now, when men upon the earth, according to the rites, make handsome sacrifices, and entreat the Gods for favour, Hekate is called."*[64]

Considering the all embracing nature of this universal Goddess, you would be forgiven for thinking that it is not necessary to work with or understand the nature of other Gods and Goddesses associated with Hekate. But as we have already said, other than Hesiod's *Theogony*, Hekate has no surviving mythology of her own; instead her appearances are as a supporting actress in the myths and legends of the other Gods.

As a result it would be easy to assume that she is syncretic with Legba of the Voudou traditions, a gate-keeper necessary to gain access to the other entities; but do not fall into this trap, for whilst their roles are similar in certain aspects they are entirely different; although don't be surprised if one should take an interest in you as a result of contact with the other.

So whilst Hekate is a Goddess of the crossroads and is both the guardian and mistress of the dead, her other aspects are very diverse and very powerful, which may be why Hesiod considered her worthy of calling alongside other, more popular deities. A brief overview of the deities she is most closely connected to follows and should serve as a foundation should you ever wish to evoke Hekate alongside other deities.

ZEUS

The Olympian Sky God Zeus was the son of the Titans Kronos and Rhea. Kronos, as the result of a prophecy issued by Gaia and Uranus which foresaw his downfall by the hand of one of his offspring, swallowed each child his wife bore him. Desolate Rhea devised a way of tricking Kronos by presenting him a rock in blankets rather than a child and Zeus was hidden from his father. Once fully grown Zeus fulfils the prophecy and overthrows his father and becomes the supreme God.

The main connection with Hekate comes from Hesiod's *Theogony*, where he states that she is honoured by Zeus and not only given her due portion of the earth, sea and sky after the Titanic war but also additional jurisdiction over the young and childbirth. This *'honouring'* may be the reason that in lesser known works Zeus and Asteria are named as Hekate's parents instead.

Although primarily considered a sky God who wielded thunder and lightning, his roles were many, he was considered a protector against evil and of property, an avenger of misdeeds, the guardian of secrets and sacred oaths and even a guardian of women who lay in childbirth; many attributes which are shared with Hekate.

---

[64] Theogony, Hesiod, C8th BCE.

POSEIDON

Also the offspring of Kronos and Rhea, Poseidon was born before Zeus and was swallowed by Kronos but later regurgitated by the Titan God. He is the God of the sea, storms and earthquakes, which he creates by smashing rocks with his trident. Some also considered him responsible for the creation of the horse.

His connection with Hekate also originates with the *Theogony* of Hesiod, Hekate is said to be benevolent to horsemen, an attribute she shares with Poseidon, but also fishermen and those that traverse the sea are looked upon favourably if they pray to Hekate and Poseidon together.

A much more tenuous link but one worthy of some consideration is one of the lovers that Poseidon takes. Pausanias writes of a story from Arcadia, which tells of the time when Demeter roamed the earth searching for Persephone. Poseidon lusting after her followed, and she took flight in the form of the horse and hid amongst a herd of mares, Poseidon saw this and turned himself into a stallion and mated with her, the offspring of the union were an immortal horse and a Goddess whose name could not be mentioned to the uninitiated, but who was named instead Despoina meaning *'mistress'*; an epithet which was shared by both Artemis and Hekate.

HERMES

Normally purported to be the son of Zeus and Maia, Hermes is most often considered to be the messenger of the Gods, and more specifically Zeus himself. The mythology surrounding his early life is interesting, he escaped his cradle and stole Apollo's cattle and even denied this act of thievery in front of Zeus himself, but as a result of inventing the lyre he escaped Apollo's wrath and became his friend and messenger.

One of the Homeric hymns to Hermes claims he is full of tricks, a thief, a spy, a bringer of dreams and a watcher at the gate; he is often also considered to be a guide of the dead. In another hymn he is considered a bringer of good luck; and the invention of divination using dice is also attributed to him.

He is again mentioned in the *Theogony* as being called alongside Hekate specifically in relation to increasing livestock; however his roles as the watcher at the gate and guide of the dead are remarkably similar to those Hekate subsequently inherits in later times. As messenger of the Gods he is intrinsically linked to the mysteries of Demeter and Persephone as it was Hermes who was sent to sweet talk Hades into allowing Persephone to return to her Mother. Porphyry also mentions Hermes and Hekate being honoured together in personal rites, and the *Greek Magical Papyri* conflate Hermes and Hekate together in a number of fragments.

HELIOS

Helios is another Titan God whose parents were normally considered to be Hyperion and Theia; he is the brother of Selene. As the God of the sun he rode a chariot across the sky drawn by fiery horses during the day, whilst his sister drove another chariot sometimes said to be drawn by horses, sometimes bulls, across the skies during the night. He was considered capable of teaching witches the power of the evil eye.

He, along with Hekate is the only one to witness the abduction of Persephone to the underworld and this may be the source of the syncretisation with Selene who rode the heavens in opposition to her brother, for Hekate only heard Persephone's cries as she was residing in her cave, which could have been a metaphor for the night realms in which Selene resides, or even the cave in which her unconscious lover Endymion slumbers peacefully for eternity.

He is also undeniably linked with the most famous of the Thessalian witches and Priestesses of Hekate; Medea who was his granddaughter, in Ovid's *Metamorphoses* she evokes both Hekate and Helios together as a result of her love for Jason; also Kirke, who in some myths is his daughter and in others she is the offspring of Hekate and Aeetes.

DIONYSUS

A God of liberation, wine, fertility and agriculture Dionysus has, much like Hekate herself, a slightly sketchy history, although his integration into the Olympian pantheon is much more complete, there are some scholars that believe he was originally a foreign God adopted into the Olympian mythology.

The main argument for this seems to be based upon the story and foreign location of his birth. Zeus having fallen in love with a human girl impregnated her with a Thunderbolt; he then removed the foetal child from her womb to protect them both from the wrath of Hera, and sewed him up in his thigh and took him to Nysa where he was born.

This connection with Nysa and the older Thracian and Cretan Gods Sabazios and Zagreus, lead some to believe that Dionysus and Hades may have had a common origin, which would certainly go some way to explaining the connection with the Eleusinian Mystery Cult, of which Hekate is also a part.

They are also linked together along with Apollo, Demeter and the Mousai as having jurisdiction over Bacchic, orgiastic or initiatory rites. And although a God in his own right, it is interesting to note that he petitioned Hekate for her help in magickal rites.

DEMETER

Another Titan and offspring of Kronos and Rhea, Demeter is the Goddess of fertility, grain, marriage and teaching the mysteries to mankind, the latter of which came about as the result of the abduction of her daughter Persephone by Hades the God of the underworld.

The Homeric hymn to Demeter states that when no other deity could tell of the abduction of her daughter by Hades, Hekate came forward to say what she had heard. Euripides actually suggests in his *Tragedy Ion*, that the Athenians believed Hekate to be the offspring of Demeter which would tie in with the connection with Poseidon as noted earlier. Hekate's connection thickens as there is an ancient painting, mentioned by Kerenyi,[65] depicting

---

[65] Eleusis Archetypal Image of Mother and Daughter, Kerenyi, 1967.

Hekate and Iakkhos, which is believed to be a young Dionysus leading the soon to be initiates to the temple of Demeter at Eleusis.

PERSEPHONE

An Olympian Goddess, Persephone is the Daughter of Demeter and Zeus and the wife to Hades. Upon her return to her mother from the underworld, Persephone is embraced by Hekate who becomes her constant companion.

Although from time to time she is lauded as a Goddess of spring and new growth in most mythologies she is known as the Queen of the Underworld, in this guise she could be both benevolent and vengeful.

In one myth the witch Kirke who we have already mentioned because of her possible familial relationship with Hekate instructs Odysseus on how to enter the realm of Persephone and Hades, the underworld. The Cumaean Sybil also performs a similar rite involving Hekate and Persephone to access the underworld and as a result, she, like Hekate is often attributed with the rites of necromancy. Homer states that she is capable of creating curses, and Nonnus claimed that she was the Queen of Ghosts, and the *Greek Magical Papyri* regularly conflate both Hekate and Persephone together.

APOLLO

Unlike the other deities mentioned so far, Apollo has no direct mythological or literary connection with Hekate, but is included here as the result of circumstantial evidence. Another of the offspring of Zeus, Apollo and his sister Artemis were also children of Leto, the Goddess of childbirth. Leto's own sister was Asteria who is most commonly recognised as Hekate's mother, which effectively makes Hekate, Apollo and Artemis cousins. In later times Artemis and Hekate also became syncretised and the playwright Euripides even named Hekate as a daughter of Leto, one assumes as a result of this merging.

More importantly perhaps is his connection with Helios, by the time of Pausanias, many agreed that Helios and Apollo were one and the same, and anthropologists surmise that they may have both derived from an earlier, now forgotten deity. As a result many of his attributes are similar to Helios. He is also considered the God of prophecy, healing, averting of evil and overseer to the young, which makes him eminently compatible with Hekate.

ANUBIS

> *"Maiden, I beg you to be present at these sacred rites. Ever with a gladsome heart and ever gracious to the Oxherd"*[66]

A little like Apollo, Anubis is a rank outsider when it comes to literary connections with Hekate, however the two sources that possibly include him are too interesting to ignore. Anubis' parentage is sometimes listed as Re and Nephthys, other times Osiris and Nephthys, he was originally the God of the Underworld but in later times became associated more with the burial of

---

[66] The Goddess Hekate, Ronan, 1992.

the dead and guiding souls to the underworld, which of course is a role he shares in common with Hekate.

And although an Egyptian deity, at least by the time of the *Greek Magical Papyri* and possibly anything up to six centuries earlier in the Orphic Cults, and it is in these texts that the interesting anomaly that crops up.

The Orphic hymn to Hekate states in certain, although not all, translations that she is *'gracious to the Oxherd'*, there have been a number of speculations regarding this over the years, with it being posited that Orpheus himself is the Oxherd because he charmed the bovine like race of unsophisticated men with his lyre and songs, however, Anubis is given the epithet of Oxherd in at least four of the *Greek Magical Papyri* and Demotic texts.

Now, it shouldn't be forgotten that by the time of the *Greek Magical Papyri*, Anubis had been syncretised with Hermes and took on a number of his roles; being known as Hermanubis, but why was this? Does is hark back to an older association through the Orphic mystery cult? Whatever the reasons, when you also consider the connection between Hermes and Hekate already in existence, we now have a subtle but interesting relationship between these two deities.

II - OTHER MAGICKAL CREATURES

Nymphs - Nymphs were female nature spirits or sometimes minor Goddesses in Greek mythology; apart from often being the object of one of the male Olympian Gods' affections and indiscretions, their main function was as guardians of specific objects or places, such as rivers, lakes, trees, plants, mountains and caves. There were a few Nymphs that were tied to towns and urban dwellings, spirits of place and home as it were. The sheer number of these beings is almost beyond counting, but below are a few which have some form of association with Hekate either directly or through a deity that she is connected with or has been syncretised with.

The Dryads – This is the collective name for nymphs of the trees and forests, they were further sub divided into sub groups according to the species of tree or plant that they had guardianship over. Nymphs may have heralded the coming of Hekate much as the sounds of barking dogs were also supposed to have signified the Goddess' presence.

The Lampades – These are nymphs of the underworld and were often associated with Hekate, they could be identified by the torches that they carried. Their purpose is sometimes considered to be guides of the Mystai in the Eleusinian mysteries.

The Lamia – demonic underworld nymphs who normally manifested as a beautiful woman, they were considered part of the retinue of Hekate and their purpose was to steal the souls of children and handsome young men, possibly the origins of the Succubus in later times. One specific Lamia was the Queen Lamia Lybis who was beloved by Zeus, to punish her Hera stole her children, in her rage at this atrocity, Lamia turned into a child eating demon.

The parallels between this and the story of Lilith are interesting. Lilith being the first wife of Adam, who according to some mythologies refused to be subservient and deserted him, she subsequently mated with *'demonic'* entities but as punishment for her desertion God killed every one of her offspring so she took to hunting the first born males of humanity.

The Naiades – Nymphs of fresh water, some were considered the handmaidens of Kirke who was a priestess (and sometimes daughter) of Hekate. Nymphs may have heralded the coming of Hekate.

The Okeanides – The daughters of Okeanos, these were also fresh water nymphs but their remit was not only to stand as guardians of these water sources on the earthly realms but also the water of the air as well, such as mist and rain, Sixty of them became part of the retinue of Artemis, who we know became syncretised with Hekate in later times.

Skylla – A sea nymph who was transformed into a monster by a jealous Kirke (mentioned above). In some mythologies she is also considered to be the offspring of Hekate.

III - CORRESPONDENCES

Pick up any book of correspondences and you are assaulted with a wealth of information; lists and lists of items categorised, grouped and ordered according to any number of seemingly arbitrary criteria, and almost without fail there is little explanation as to why certain animals, perfumes, deities, colours and whatnot are given a specific attribute.

But the knowledge and use of these associations and sympathetic items such as herbs and incenses can enrich practise and ritual immeasurably. Therefore the following pages contain a comprehensive (although not exhaustive) list of correspondences that the reader may use and experiment with, but also a brief explanation either of a personal gnosis or an academic nature, wherever possible, many of these correspondences have foundation with the *Greek Magical Papyri* and were derived using the English translation by Betz; where the actual identity of the Goddess is unknown or there may be a syncretisation of a number of Goddesses which include Hekate, this has been stated.

SYMBOLS AND OTHER SACRED OBJECTS

ACONITE (EXTREMELY TOXIC)

This was listed in the *Argonautica Orphica* as one of the herbs in the Garden of Hekate which was purported to have been situated in Colchis near the palace of Aeetes, it was protected by un-scalable walls and a dazzling light which blinded those who came near it who were not in a state of purity.

Ovid in his *Metamorphoses* claimed that Medea used Aconite in an attempt to poison her stepson; he also claimed that Aconite was formed by the drool of the three headed hound of Hades called Kerberus.

Diodorus Siculus in his *Library of History* claimed that Hekate was King Aeetes' wife and mother of both Circe and Medea; she was supposed to have discovered the poisonous properties of aconite and used it to get rid of her rivals and enemies.

ALMOND

The connection here is quite obscure, but as it is regularly quoted in popular culture as a sacred food of Hekate it has been included. The only connection appears to be through the Goddess Kybele, who was on occasion syncretised as Rhea-Hekate, in some versions of her mythology, she became pregnant with a child by Zeus; the child was a fearful daemon so the Gods cut off his genitals and from the blood an almond tree grew.

Another possible reason why the almond has also become associated with Hekate is because it is a member of the Prunus family of fruits, which also contain apricots and peaches, the kernels of which were known to produce cyanide. In several *Greek Magical Papyri* spells at least one of which calls upon Hekate a 'fruit pit' is required as the part of the spell.

BAY LEAVES

This was listed in the *Argonautica Orphica* as one of the herbs in the Garden of Hekate which was purported to have been situated in Colchis near the palace of Aeetes.

Found in Theocritus' *Idylls* where it is burnt by Simaetha as part of a love spell which invokes Hekate.

In Virgil's *Aeneid*, the Cumaean Sybil, who was placed in charge of the sacred grove at Avernus by Hekate, writes her prophecies on bay leaves.

In PGM IV.2622-2707 it is listed as an ingredient for a kyphi style incense which is formed into small *'pills'*. This a slander spell to Selene that requires an iron ring carved with an image of Hekate.

BEAR

In PGM VII.686-702, known as the Bear Charm, which is apparently for any purpose, names used such as *'Brimo'* and *'Universal Queen'* are sometimes considered epithets of Hekate, the deity evoked is also described as *'fire bodied'* and *'sharply armed'*. This is very similar to PGM IV.1331-89 which is known as the spell of the bear, which utilises, offerings found in other PGM charms which may relate to Hekate such as the fat of a goat and cumin.

BEES

Medea instructs Jason to make a libation of *'the works of bees'* in the *Argonautica* of Apollonius of Rhodes.

BELLADONNA (EXTREMELY TOXIC)

This was listed in the *Argonautica Orphica* as one of the herbs in the Garden of Hekate which was purported to have been situated in Colchis near the palace of Aeetes.

BLACK LAMBS & SHEEP

Ovid (8 CE) in his *Metamorphoses* says that Medea sacrificed two black sheep to Hekate as part of a rite to reanimate Jason's father Aeson.

Medea instructs Jason to slaughter a female sheep to Hekate to call for her help, it is not however clear if this sheep is black or not.

Aeneas is instructed by the Cumaean Sybil to slaughter a black lamb prior to summoning Hekate and gaining passage to the underworld.

Horace in *Satires 8* describes how the witches Canidia and Sagana tear a black lamb apart before calling upon Hekate.

BRONZE

In PGM IV.2241-2358 this prayer/evocation calls upon Hekate in a number of guises, it also refers to sacred or magickal symbols and passwords; *'bronze sandal'* is used as one of the passwords by the operator.

Pindar in his *Paean 2* calls Hekate the *'maiden of the ruddy feet'*; this may be a reference to her feet being stained with some form of Henna, but could possibly be a reference to bronze sandals which would certainly had a ruddy glow in torchlight. Sadly this is a fragment so you will need to exercise your own gnosis regarding this information.

CARDAMOM

This was listed in the *Argonautica Orphica* as one of the herbs in the Garden of Hekate which was purported to have been situated in Colchis near the palace of Aeetes.

CAT

PGM III.1-164 is an avenging charm which uses the body of a cat with a number of lamellae inserted into body cavities, this spell evokes Hekate, Hermes and the conflated Hermekate; it also makes reference to *'the netter'* which may be a reference to the Goddess Britomartis and also calls the Queen of Corpses.

PGM VII 756-94 A prayer to a many formed, many named Goddess, with the epithet of Mene also called the Mistress of the whole world, a long list of *'signs and symbols'* are recited which includes the word cat.

CATTLE

In PGM IV.1390-1495 dung from a black cow is listed as part of an offering in a love spell of attraction calling upon the help of fallen heroes which also evokes Hekate.

PGM IV.2006-2125 requires that a three-headed, six-armed figure of Hekate is inscribed on a flax leaf, one of which has the head of a cow.

PGM IV 2785 – 2870 is entitled *'Prayer to Selene for any Spell'* however this is most definitely a conflation of Hekate and Selene and in one section she is described as, bull headed, bull eyed and bull faced.

Lydus claims in his *Liber De Mensibus* that the head of Hekate corresponding to the element of air, is that of bull which snorts and bellows.

CAVES

Hekate emerges from a subterranean cave under Mount Avernus, when summoned by the Cumaean Sybil in Ovid's *Metamorphoses*.

Hekate dwells in a cave in the *Homeric Hymn to Demeter* and it is from here she hears the cries of Persephone as she is abducted.

CHEESE

Kirke blended cheese and barley meal together and offered it to Odysseus' crew prior to enchanting them and turning them into swine.

Athenaeus claimed that cheesecakes, specifically one called an amphiphon was taken to the crossroads on days when the sun rise and moonset coincided, these cakes were normally sacred to Artemis, but the crossroad symbolism cannot be ignored.

CINNAMON (LEAF)

In PGM IV.2622-2707, lead is listed as an ingredient for a kyphi style incense which is formed into small *'pills'*. This a slander spell to Selene that requires an iron ring carved with an image of Hekate.

CUMIN

In PGM IV.2708-84 cumin is mixed with goat fat and burnt as an offering in a love spell of attraction specifically naming Hekate.

CYPRESS

Cypress was named as one of the constituents of a funerary wreath in the *Aeneid*, which was part of a suicide rite in which Dido evokes Hekate before killing herself for the love of the hero Aeneas.

Mentioned again in the *Aeneid* as part of the rite performed to summon Hekate from the cave at mount Avernus, it is specifically mentioned as a funerary wreath; both of these references appear to be more a link with the restless dead than Hekate herself.

DAISY

Athenaeus named mullet as sacred to Hekate, and the natural assumption is that this is a fish that is being talked about, however, in the notes of an early translation of Theocritus' *Idylls* states that mullet is another name for fleabane which is from the daisy family, considering the number of spells which call for *'coded'* herbals to be used, this is something worth taking into account.

DOGS (SOMETIMES BLACK)

In Ovid's *Metamorphoses*, when Kirke (sometimes daughter of Hekate) summons the Goddess as part of a spell the sounds of dogs howling fills the air.

In Theocritus' *Idylls*, Simaetha takes the howling and barking of the town watchdogs as a sign that Hekate is coming.

In Virgil's *Aeneid*, dogs bark at the coming of Hekate when she is summoned by the Cumaean Sybil.

Euripides in his play *Hecabe*, claimed that the former queen of Troy would be transformed into a dog *'with glaring tawny eyes'*, some hundred years later, this act of metamorphoses was according to Lycophron at the will of Hekate and that Hecabe would become one of her beasts. PGM IV.1390-1495 is a love spell of attraction calling upon the help of heroes which calls upon Hekate with a number of epithets including *'O Black Bitch'*.

PGM IV.2006-2125 requires that a three headed, six armed figure of Hekate is inscribed on a flax leaf, one of which has the head of a dog.

PGM IV.2241-2358 this prayer/evocation calls upon many epithets which are known to be related to Hekate, some of which are *'O Dog in maiden form'* and *'saviour, world-wide, dog-shaped'*, also *'black dog'*.

PGM IV.2708-84 A love spell of attraction who names Hekate as *'dog leader'*.

PGM IV.2785-2890 A prayer to Selene for any spell, which specifically names Hekate states that *'fierce dogs are dear to her'* and that she has *'the voice of dogs'*.

PGM IV.2785-2890 Listed in a prayer to Selene for any spell as part of a protective charm, a lodestone should have a triple faced Hekate carved upon it the middle face is a bull horned maid, the left a dog and the right a goat.

PGM VII.756-94 A prayer to a many formed, many named Goddess, with the epithet of Mene also called the Mistress of the whole world, a long list of *'signs and symbols'* are recited which includes the word dog.

EGGS

Medea adds eggs to a noxious brew she creates for Jason to restore life to his father in Ovid's *Metamorphoses*.

FLAX

PGM IV.1390-1495 Burnt flax ashes are listed as part of an offering in love spell of attraction calling upon the help of heroes which evokes Hekate.

PGM IV.2006-2125 requires that a three headed, six armed figure of Hekate is inscribed on a flax leaf, one of which has the head of a dog.

FRANKINCENSE

PGM IV.2441-2621 Listed as an incense ingredient in a lunar spell of attraction, which calls upon a triple voiced, triple headed Selene who is also name as mistress of the three ways, light bringer and Hermes and Hekate conflated.

PGM IV.2622-2707 Listed as an ingredient for a kyphi style incense which is formed into small *'pills'*. This a slander spell to Selene that requires an iron ring carved with an image of Hekate.

PGM IV.2785-2890 Listed in a prayer to Selene for any spell as part of an incense to use given as a burnt offering.

Traditional funerary incense used by Aeneas prior to summoning Hekate from the Avernus cave as instructed by the Cumaean Sybil.

GALANGAL /GINGER

PGM IV.2441-2621 Listed as an incense ingredient in a lunar spell of attraction, which calls upon a triple voiced, triple headed Selene who is also name as mistress of the three ways, light bringer and also Hermes and Hekate conflated.

GARLIC

PGM IV.2622-2707 A single clove of garlic is required as an ingredient for kyphi style incense which is formed into small *'pills'* and stamped with an iron ring which has been inscribed with an image of Hekate.

Horace in *Odes III* claims it was garlic that Medea gave Jason to cover himself with whilst undergoing the trials to claim the Golden fleece (caution does have to be exercised though as much of Horace's work was satirical)

GRAVE DIRT (PREFERABLY FROM AN ANCIENT BATTLEFIELD)

PGM IV.1390-1495 this love spell requires the operator to go to a graveyard or battlefield, where dirt is collected, Hekate is evoked in a number of guises, three headed Goddess, Kore, lady of night and key holding Persephassa.

HONEY

See *Bees*, also honey derived products such as mead are received favourably as an offering.

Kirke offered honey to Odysseus' crew prior to enchanting them.

HORSE

PGM VII.756-94 A prayer to a many formed, many named Goddess, with the epithet of Mene also called the Mistress of the whole world, a long list of *'signs and symbols'* are recited which includes the word horse.

A selection of the *Chaldean Oracles* known as the *'Epiphany of Hekate'* states that if you call upon her often then you may see a horse flashing brightly or a child riding upon a horse's back shooting arrows.

IRON

PGM IV.2241-2358 this prayer/evocation calls upon Hekate in a number of guises, it also refers to sacred or magickal symbols and passwords; *'iron wheel'* is used as one of the passwords by the operator.

PGM IV.2622-2707 A kyphi style incense is formed into small *'pills'* and is stamped with an iron ring which has been inscribed with an image of Hekate.

JUNIPER

This was listed in the *Argonautica Orphica* as one of the herbs in the Garden of Hekate which was purported to have been situated in Colchis near the palace of Aeetes.

PGM IV.2622-2707 Listed as a burnt offering in the creation of a protective charm which is fashioned with a magnet and an image of Hekate inscribed upon it.

KEYS

The *Orphic Hymn to Hekate* specifically names her Kleidouchos which means *'key bearer'*, this may be as a result of her roles of Propylaia and Apotropais; guardian against evil and of boundaries. Often her shrines and statues were found at the entrance to homes and other temples.

PGM IV.1390-1495 A love spell of attraction calling upon the help of heroes which calls upon Hekate with a number of epithets including Key-holding Persephassa.

PGM IV.2241-2358 This prayer/evocation calls upon Hekate in a number of guises, it also refers to sacred or magickal symbols held by the operator of the spell one of which is a key.

PGM VII.756-94 A prayer to a many formed, many named Goddess, with the epithet of Mene also called the Mistress of the whole world, a long list of *'signs and symbols'* are recited which includes the word key.

LEAD

The substance used most often for the creation of *defixiones* or curse tablets, many of which have been found that call upon Hekate for help.

LION

PGM VII.756-94 A prayer to a many formed, many named Goddess, with the epithet of Mene also called the Mistress of the whole world, a long list of *'signs and symbols'* are recited which includes the word lion.

Psellus' translation of one of the fragments of the *Chaldean Oracles* claims that you can see things in *'lion form'*, later scholars are now contesting this translation, so you will have to exercise some personal gnosis on this matter.

MAGNETS/LODESTONE

PGM IV.2622-2707 Listed in the creation of a protective charm which is fashioned with a magnet and an image of Hekate inscribed upon it.

PGM IV.2785-2890 Listed in a prayer to Selene for any spell as part of a protective charm, a lodestone should have a triple faced Hekate carved upon it the middle face is a bull horned maid, the left a dog and the right a goat.

MANDRAKE

This was listed in the *Argonautica Orphica* as one of the herbs in the Garden of Hekate which was purported to have been situated in Colchis near the palace of Aeetes.

MEAD

As an alcoholic drink derived from honey this serves as an excellent Eucharistic drink during rites and as a libation.

MUGWORT

Is considered an excellent herb to aid in vision work and trance mediumship, burned as an incense during ritual to Hekate it seems to enhance skrying and other forms of divination as well.

MUSHROOMS (NORMALLY OF THE PSYCHOTROPIC KIND)

Some academics have considered the possibility of the sacred drink Kykeon containing traces of psychotropics gained from various fungi, psilocybin being the prime contenders, devotees have reported excellent results when providing mushrooms as an offering especially during Deipnon (Hekate Supper).

MULLET

A first century writer Athenaeus claimed that the red mullet was sacred to Hekate, and there are other references to mullet being offered at shrines.

MYRRH

PGM IV.2441-2621 Listed as an incense ingredient in a Lunar spell of attraction, which calls upon a triple voiced, triple headed Selene who is also named as mistress of the three ways, light bringer and Hermes and Hekate conflated.

PGM IV.2785-2890 Listed in a prayer to Selene for any spell as part of an incense to use given as a burnt offering.

MYRTLE

PGM IV.2622-2707 Listed as an ingredient for a kyphi style incense which is formed into small *'pills'*. This a slander spell to Selene that requires an iron ring carved with an image of Hekate.

ONIONS

PGM IV.2441-2621 Listed as an incense ingredient in a Lunar spell of attraction, which calls upon a triple voiced, triple headed Selene who is also name as mistress of the three ways, light bringer and Hermes and Hekate conflated.

PENNYROYAL

This was listed in the *Argonautica Orphica* as one of the herbs in the Garden of Hekate which was purported to have been situated in Colchis near the palace of Aeetes.

Pennyroyal is believed to be one of the ingredients of the sacred rink Kykeon which was consumed by the initiates of the Eleusinian mysteries which it is believed Hekate is a part of.

PEPPER

This was listed in the *Argonautica Orphica* as one of the herbs in the Garden of Hekate which was purported to have been situated in Colchis near the palace of Aeetes. It was specifically Ethiopian Pepper.

POPPY

This was listed in the *Argonautica Orphica* as one of the herbs in the Garden of Hekate which was purported to have been situated in Colchis near the palace of Aeetes.

Ovid in his *Metamorphoses* stated that the drug given to Jason by Medea to send the dragon guarding the Golden Fleece was a form of opium.

RED WINES

In Virgil's *Aeneid*; the Cumaean Sybil pours libations of wine upon the heads of three bulls whilst summoning Hekate.

SAFFRON

This was listed in the *Argonautica Orphica* as one of the herbs in the Garden of Hekate which was purported to have been situated in Colchis near the palace of Aeetes.

Hekate is described as wearing a *'saffron veil'* in the *Orphic Hymn to Hekate*.

PGM IV.2441-2621 Listed as an incense ingredient in a Lunar spell of attraction, which calls upon a triple voiced, triple headed Selene who is also name as mistress of the three ways, light bringer and Hermes and Hekate conflated.

SAGE

PGM IV.2785-2890 Listed in a prayer to Selene for any spell as part of an incense to use given as a burnt offering.

SANDALS

PGM IV.2241-2358 this prayer/evocation calls upon Hekate in a number of guises, it also refers to sacred or magickal symbols held by the operator of the spell one of which is a sandal. Again later the words *'bronze sandal'* is used as part of a password by the operator.

SANDALWOOD

PGM LXX.4-25 Used as an ingredient in a cake created to cause insomnia in a person, which is found as part of the charm to Hekate-Erischigal.

SESAME

This was listed in the *Argonautica Orphica* as one of the herbs in the Garden of Hekate which was purported to have been situated in Colchis near the palace of Aeetes.

PGM LXX.4-25 Scattered as part of an apotropaic charm to Hekate-Erischigal.

SNAKES

In Ovid's *Metamorphoses*, when Kirke (sometimes daughter of Hekate) summons the Goddess as part of a spell the ground seethes with black snakes.

Horace in his *Satires 8* states that after Hekate is evoked snakes *'roam at large'*. And they bury the *'fangs of a spotted snake'* as part of their spell.

PGM IV.1390-1495 A love spell of attraction calling upon the help of heroes which attributes Hekate with a number of epithets including *'Child girt with fiery serpents'*.

PGM IV.2785-2890 A prayer to Selene for any spell, which specifically names Hekate and describes her as both, having fearful snakes upon her forehead and rows of serpents down her back.

PGM VII.756-94 A prayer to a many formed, many named Goddess, with the epithet of Mene also called the Mistress of the whole world, a long list of *'signs and symbols'* are recited which includes the word serpent.

STORAX

PGM III.1-164 Storax is burnt as a fumigation in the ritual of the cat, which was considered good for any purpose, restraining charioteers in races, bringing dreams, binding and love charms. This spell evokes Hekate, Hermes and the conflated Hermekate; it also makes reference to *'the netter'* which may be a reference to the Goddess Britomartis.

PGM IV.2441-2621 Listed as an incense ingredient in a Lunar spell of attraction, which calls upon a triple voiced, triple headed Selene who is also named as mistress of the three ways, light bringer and Hermes and Hekate conflated.

PGM IV.2622-2707 Listed as a burnt offering in the creation of a protective charm which is fashioned with a magnet and an image of Hekate inscribed upon it.

PGM IV.2785-2890 Listed in a prayer to Selene for any spell as part of an incense to use given as a burnt offering.

Muller-Ebeling et al. (see footnotes) provide an incense recipe which is purported to be from late Antiquity (3rd century CE), sadly the source in unclear, however storax is given as a key ingredient. This may be because the *Orphic Hymn to Prothyraea*, who Proclus believed was synonymous with Hekate, used a fumigation of storax as the incense.

SULPHUR

Ovid in his *Metamorphoses* says that Medea used sulphur as part of a set of purifications in a rite evoking to Hekate to reanimate Jason's father Aeson.

SWORD

PGM IV.2241-2358 this prayer/evocation calls upon many epithets which are known to be related to Hekate, one which is not specifically obvious is *'O crested one, who draw swords'*.

THE NUMBER 3

Hekate has numerous associations with the number 3, not least that she is often named in various *Greek Magical Papyri* fragments as thrice bound, triple pointed, triple faced, three headed, three voiced, and mistress of the three ways.

In Theocritus' *Idylls*, Simaetha as part of a love spell which evokes Hekate pours three libations and makes three prayers to the Goddess.

PGM IV.1390-1495 A love spell of attraction calling upon the help of heroes which calls upon Hekate, the rite is to be performed for three consecutive days.

THE NUMBER 7

PGM III.1-164 Seven lamps are lit in the ritual of the cat, which was considered good for any purpose, restraining charioteers in races, bringing dreams, binding and love charms, it also makes reference to *'the netter'* which may be a reference to the Goddess Britomartis and the Queen of Corpses.

THREE WAY CROSS ROADS

Hekate was known to have a number of epithets (names) associated with Crossroads, including Trioditis and Trivia, both of which in essence mean *'of the three ways'*. Hekate Trivia however was most likely a conflation of Hekate and the Roman Goddess Trivia whose story parallels that of Hekate's role in the story of Demeter and Persephone.

PGM IV.1390-1495 A love spell of attraction calling upon the help of heroes which calls upon Hekate with a number of epithets including *'Lady of the Crossroads'*.

PGM IV.2708-84 in a love spell of attraction specifically naming Hekate, she is regaled as being a *'crossroad'* Goddess and as one who *'oft frequent the triple way'*.

TORCHES

Known epithets of Hekate relating to torches are Phosphoros – meaning *'light bringer'*, and more specifically Dadophoros – which literally means *'torch-bearer'*.

The *Homeric Hymn to Demeter* states that Hekate came to Demeter on the tenth morning after Persephone disappeared, holding a torch.

PGM IV.2708-84 in a love spell of attraction specifically naming Hekate, she is regaled as being *'torch-bearing'*.

PGM.VII 756-94 A prayer to a many formed, many named Goddess, with the epithet of Mene also called the Mistress of the whole world, a long list of *'signs and symbols'* are recited which includes the word torch.

WHEAT & BARLEY

Wheat Bran & Barley were sprinkled onto the fire by Simaetha whilst summoning Hekate in Theocritus' *Idylls II*.

PGM IV.1390-1495 this love spell requires the operator to go to a graveyard or battlefield, where seven pieces of bread are left as offering to chthonic Hermes, chthonic Hekate and other underworld attendant spirits.

PGM IV.2708-84 in a love spell of attraction specifically naming Hekate, she is regaled as being the *'guard and shelter of the threshing floor'*.

WORMWOOD

PGM IV.2622-2707 A single stem which has been picked at sunrise is required as an ingredient for kyphi style incense which is formed into small *'pills'* and stamped with an iron ring which has been inscribed with an image of Hekate.

YEW

This was listed in the *Argonautica Orphica* as one of the herbs in the Garden of Hekate which was purported to have been situated in Colchis near the palace of Aeetes.

IV - ELEMENTAL ATTRIBUTIONS

The table given below is a timeline of readily accessible literary references to Hekate that contain obvious elemental attributions which can be used to aid in ritual construction, elemental meditation or even just helping to write devotional hymns with an elemental theme. It must however be stated that, whilst the following attributions roughly follow fairly standard formulas which can be checked in something like Crowley's *777* or Skinner's *Complete Magicians Tables,* you the reader must bear in mind that the purpose of this project as a whole is not to mindlessly regurgitate something already in existence or even to faithfully reconstruct something long lost, but to grow and develop a real and living tradition, therefore please remember that these are works of personal gnosis so it will be up to the individual reader to explore these references and draw their own conclusions.

Date	Source	Earth	Air	Fire	Water
8th - 7th Century BCE	Hesiod, Theogony	✓	✓		✓
7th Century BCE	Homeric Hymn to Demeter	✓		✓	
7th Century BCE	Alkman, Fragment 63			✓	
5th Century BCE	Aeschylus, Fragment 249 (quoted by Porphyry in On Superstition)	✓			
5th Century BCE	Hippocrates, On the Sacred Disease	✓			
5th Century BCE	Sophocles, The Root Cutters (cited by Ronan, The Goddess Hekate)	✓			
5th Century BCE	Sophron, The Women who say they will expel the Goddess	✓		✓	
462 BCE	Pindar, Pythian Odes 4		✓		
450 BCE	Aeschylus, The Choephori	✓			
431 BCE	Euripides, Medea			✓	
412 BCE	Euripides, Helen	✓	✓	✓	
3rd Century BCE	Apollonius of Rhodes, Argonautica	✓		✓	
3rd Century BCE	Lycophron, Alexandria	✓		✓	✓
270 BCE	Theocritus, Idylls			✓	
2nd Century BCE onwards	Greek Magical Papyri	✓		✓	✓
1st Century BCE	Virgil, The Aeneid	✓	✓		
35 BCE	Horace, Satires	✓			
30 BCE	Horace, Epodes		✓		
8 CE	Ovid, Metamorphoses	✓	✓	✓	✓
1st Century CE	Seneca, Medea	✓		✓	✓
1st Century CE	Statius, Thebaid			✓	

1st – 3rd Century CE	Orphic Hymn to Hekate	✓	✓		✓
2nd Century CE	Plutarch, Roman Questions	✓			
2nd Century CE	Pausanias, Description of Greece		✓	✓	
2nd Century CE	Lucian, Philopseudes	✓	✓		
2nd Century CE	Chaldean Oracles, K19, K28, K29, K45 (Kroll referencing)	✓	✓	✓	
2nd Century CE	Apuleius, Metamorphoses	✓	✓		✓
3rd Century CE	Hippolytus, Philosophumena	✓	✓	✓	
3rd Century CE	Porphyry, On Images	✓	✓	✓	
3rd Century CE	Porphyry, Prophecy from Oracles	✓	✓	✓	
4th Century CE	Eusebius, Praeparatio Evangelica		✓		
5th Century CE	Nonnus, Dionysiaca			✓	
5th Century CE	Macrobius, Saturnalia	✓			
6th Century CE	John Lydus, Liber de Mensibus	✓	✓	✓	✓
16th Century CE	Agrippa, Three Books of Occult Philosophy (quoting Porphyry)	✓	✓		✓

V - CALCULATING PLANETARY HOURS

Firstly we need to understand that each day is assigned to a particular classical planet; the English language does not lend itself particularly well to remembering which day corresponds to which, but a quick examination and memorisation of the French days of the week makes it clearer. The weekend days are a little more obscure as they are derived from the old Latin of Sabbath Day and Lords Day but if you have the rest down pat it shouldn't be too hard to remember the last two planets.

Monday	Lundi	Lunar/Moon Day
Tuesday	Mardi	Mars Day
Wednesday	Mercredi	Mercury Day
Thursday	Jeudi	Jupiter Day
Friday	Vendredi	Venus Day
Saturday	Samedi	Saturn/Sabbath Day
Sunday	Dimanche	Sun/Lords Day

Now we are aware of the assignments for the Classical planets, we need to consider our purpose, not only to decide the day on which to perform our work be it a form of divination or a more ritualistic action.

Once we know how long our planetary hours are, we can assign them to the correct planets, sadly the order of planets is not the same as the days of the week, but hey nobody ever said this magick stuff was going to be easy. The order is as follows:

Saturn	Jupiter	Mars	Sun	Venus	Mercury	Moon

The example we used in the main body of the book with a sunrise of 05:52 and a sunset of 20:33 was a Tuesday, so the planetary ruler for that day is Mars, so the first hour of that day is assigned to Mars, the second to the Sun, third to Venus and so forth, you then cycle through until all 12 hours have a planet as seen below, for the ease of calculation the seconds have been rounded down which accounts for the small discrepancy at the end of the day however you may wish to be more accurate in your own calculations:

Hour 1	05:52	Mars
Hour 2	07:05:20	Sun
Hour 3	08:18:40	Venus
Hour 4	09:32	Mercury
Hour 5	10:45:20	Moon
Hour 6	11:58:40	Saturn

Hour 7	13:12	Jupiter
Hour 8	14:25:20	Mars
Hour 9	15:38:40	Sun
Hour 10	16:52	Venus
Hour 11	18:05:20	Mercury
Hour 12	19:18:40	Moon

So what we eventually come up with is a suitable day of the week, with a suitable time of the day (two in fact) where we are most closely aligned with the purpose of our work. Of course it will become more complicated when you take in the divinatory timetable into account so it is worth stating that this method is best suited to less everyday work, unless you are particularly masochistic, dedicated, or both!

VI - REDUCTION SIGILS

I first came across the concept of the reduction sigil from studying the works of ritual magicians inspired by Austin Osman Spare. Although Spare made reduction sigils popular, they appear centuries earlier in *The Three Books of Occult Philosophy* of Cornelius Agrippa, published 1531-33.

Reduction sigils are deceptively simple magickal devices which sound way more complicated than they are, but in essence they are just a cut down version of a statement of intent, for example:

"I wish Temple of Hekate to be the bestselling book about Hekate for all time"

Once you have taken the statement of intent, you remove all repeating letters, like this:

"I wish Temple of ~~Hekate to~~ be ~~the bestselling~~ ~~book about Hekate for all time~~"

This leaves you with the letters:

"IWSHTEMPLOFKABSNGU"

You could of course leave it like that for the purpose of creating a magickal Lamellae or you could take it even further creating a sigil based upon these letters, like so:

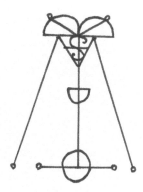

If you look carefully every letter is traceable; these sigils can be made as fancy or as plain as you like and are very effective.

GLOSSARY OF TERMS

Apotropaic – an item or action that is intended to ward off or repel malevolent spirits or actions.

Asperge – a process of purification through the sprinkling of consecrated water.

Bacchic Rites – mystery rites dedicated to the Roman God Bacchus who bore many similarities to the Greek God Dionysus; the rites were often frenzied trance like and decidedly orgiastic.

Chthonic – generally taken to mean anything that dwells within or under the earth.

Circumambulation – the act of walking around the circle whilst consecrating it.

Classical Era – a period of time within the Greco-Roman world that spanned roughly from the 8th century BCE through to the early half of the 3rd century BCE

Fumigation – as an offering this involved the use of incenses to provide fragrant smoke for the Gods.

Greek Magical Papyri – a collection of magickal texts thought to originate from ancient Greece and Egypt, it is also sometimes referred to as the PGM.

Hellenic Era – a period of time within the Greco-Roman world that spanned from the early half of the 3rd century BCE to around 30 BCE.

Kykeon – a sacred drink served to the initiates at Eleusis, it may have contained barley water and pennyroyal.

Lamellae – a thin plate or tablet, within the context of this work, it refers to slips of tin, gold, silver and lead used to inscribe magickal charms for a number of purposes.

Liminal – the point between different states or planes of existence, for example dusk is a liminal time for it is neither night nor day.

Mycenaean Era – a period of time during the Bronze Age, this ranged from approximately 1600 BCE through to 1100 BCE.

Pantheon – derived from the Greek word *pan* meaning *'all'*, a pantheon is a collection of all the Gods of a particular culture or ethnic group.

Phylactery – a magical amulet normally worn about the body to protect the magician during their work.

Polis – a city state in ancient Greece, with local government and public amenities.

Strophalos – a brass device described by philosopher Psellus, it was supposed to have contained a sapphire or stone made of lapis lazuli and was spun to evoke daemons; it is sometimes also called a Hekate's wheel or top.

Syncretised – reconciliation or merging of different beliefs, or deities.

Voces Magicae - powerful or sacred words used within magical rites, some of these are known as barbarous words because the meaning or origin is unknown.

BIBLIOGRAPHY

Agrippa, H.C. & Donald Tyson (ed) (1992) *Three Books of Occult Philosophy.* Minnesota, Llewellyn

Apollonius of Rhodes, & Richard Hunter (trans) (2009) *Jason and the Golden Fleece (The Argonautica).* Oxford, Oxford Classics

Betz, Hans Dieter (ed) (1992) *The Greek Magical Papyri in Translation.* Chicago, University of Chicago Press

Burkert, William (2004) *Greek Religion: Archaic and Classical.* Oxford, Blackwell Publishing Ltd

Clarke, Emma (ed) (2003) *Iamblichus: De Mysteriis.* Atlanta, Society of Biblical Literature

Copenhaver, Brian P. (1995) *Hermetica: The Greek Corpus Hermeticum and the Latin Asclepius in a New English Translation.* Cambridge, Cambridge University Press.

Crowley, Aleister (1998) *Book 4.* Maine, Weiser.

d'Este, Sorita (ed) (2010) *Hekate Her Sacred Fires.* London, Avalonia.

d'Este, Sorita (ed) (2006) *Hekate - Keys to the Crossroads.* London, Avalonia.

d'Este, Sorita & David Rankine (2009) *Hekate Liminal Rites.* London, Avalonia

Euripides & Philip Vellacott (trans) (1954) *The Bacchae & Other Plays.* London, Penguin.

Ginzburg, Carlo (1992) *The Night Battles: Witchcraft & Agrarian Cults in the Sixteenth & Seventeenth Century.* Maryland, Johns Hopkins University Press.

Green, Marian (1993) *Practical Techniques of Modern Magic.* Leicestershire, Thoth.

Hesiod, & Theognis, & Wender, D. (trans) (1976) *Theogony, Works and Days, and Elegies.* London, Penguin.

Homer, & H. Rieu & E. Rieu & Peter Jones (trans) (2003) *The Odyssey.* London, Penguin.

Johnston, Sarah Iles (2008) *Ancient Greek Divination.* Oxford, Wiley-Blackwell.

Johnston, Sarah Iles (1990) *Hekate Soteira.* Atlanta, Scholars Press

Kerenyi, Carl (1967) *Eleusis: Archetypal Image of Mother and Daughter.* New Jersey, Princeton University Press.

Lossky, Vladimir (1976) *The Mystical Theology of the Eastern Church.* New York, St Vladimir's Seminary Press

Lowe, J.E. (2003) *Magic in Greek and Latin Literature.* Montana, Kessinger.

Mead, G.R.S. (2010) *The Chaldean Oracles.* Montana, Kessinger.

Muller-Ebeling, Claudia et al. (2003) *Witchcraft Medicine: Healing Arts, Shamanic Practices, and Forbidden Plants.* Vermont, Inner Traditions

Ogden, Daniel (2002) *Witchcraft and Ghosts in the Greek and Roman Worlds.* Oxford, Oxford University Press.

Ovid, A.D. Melville & E.J. Kenney (trans) (2009) *Metamorphoses*. Oxford, Oxford Classics.

Pausanias & Peter Levi (trans) (1984) *Description of Greece Volume One*. London, Penguin.

Peterson, Joseph H. (2008) *John Dee's Five Books of Mystery*. Maine, Weiser.

Pinch, Geraldine (1994) *Magic in Ancient Egypt*. London, British Museum Press.

Plato (1997) *The Complete Works of Plato*. Indianapolis, Hackett.

Ronan, Stephen (ed) (1992) *The Goddess Hekate*. Hastings, Chthonios Books

Shakespeare, William (1997) *Hamlet*. London, Wordsworth

Skinner, Stephen & David Rankine (2008) *The Veritable Key of Solomon*. Singapore, Golden Hoard.

Taylor, Thomas (1995) *Hymns and Initiations*. Wiltshire, The Prometheus Trust.

INDEX

Lightning Source UK Ltd.
Milton Keynes UK
UKHW030257301018
331417UK00015B/564/P